HEART MUSIC

Poems

By Edward V. Van Slambrouck

Edited by Margo LaGattuta

iUniverse, Inc.
New York Bloomington Shanghai

HEART MUSIC
Poems

iUniverse books may be ordered through booksellers or by contacting:

iUniverse
1663 Liberty Drive
Bloomington, IN 47403
www.iuniverse.com
1-800-Authors (1-800-288-4677)

Because of the dynamic nature of the Internet, any Web addresses or links contained in this book may have changed since publication and may no longer be valid.

The views expressed in this work are solely those of the author and do not necessarily reflect the views of the publisher, and the publisher hereby disclaims any responsibility for them.

ISBN: 978-0-595-47860-6

Printed in the United States of America

For my children and grandchildren

*Poetry is the music of thought,
conveyed to us in the music
of language.*

Paul Chatfield 1779–1849
(pseudonym of Horace Smith)

CONTENTS

ACKNOWLEDGMENTS

Six key individuals have aided me with their wisdom and guidance in the task of writing and producing *Heart Music*. I thank them with as much sincerity as a human can give. They are:

poet Margo La Gattuta, M.F.A., who is the finest teacher I know. I do not know how to praise this gifted poet enough. Thus let it be known that I am indeed lucky to find such a bright person to help me. Please read "About the Editor" on page 171 for more about Margo. I also thank my brother, Dr. Paul F. Van Slambrouck, Ph.D., who provided an abundance of guidance and encouragement; my dear friend and mentor, Dr. Leonard Lutwack, Ph.D., Professor Emeritus of English of the University of Maryland, who has read many of my poems and commented with kind advice. Professor Lutwack died on April 1, 2008 at age 91. He had an illustrious academic career and was widely published. He is missed.

Also, I wish to thank fellow poets, James Ahearn and Shirley Steinman, who graciously have aided me by suggesting changes and giving guidance for many of the poems in *Heart Music*. In addition, I thank Mr. Earl Newman, my artist friend, who designed the model for the front cover of *Heart Music*. Please read "About the Artist" on page 173 for more about Earl, and last, but for goodness sake not least, my wife and love, Diane, M.A., who read much of my raw poetry and provided a more balanced vision of an idea or a word texture, which enabled me to create better poems.

Poems published elsewhere that are reprinted in *Heart Music* are:
"Bastogne"—*Gazette van Detroit*,
"Birds Flock"—*Tierra Verde News*,
"Class of 1948"—*FOCUS*,
"Smithery," "High Stepping" and "When I Write My Wild Poems"—all published in *Peninsula Poets*.

INTRODUCTION

Sidney Lanier once said, "Music is love in search of a word." In *Heart Music*, Edward Van Slambrouck has found that word and many more. These are poems inspired by his deep love of music and his celebration of life in all its glories and sorrows. From his experiences as a son, father, husband, citizen and spiritual being, he has woven a collection of powerful poems that sing to the heart and bring us closer to understanding our own lives.

He says in the title poem, "Heart Music," "Music in the chamber of the veins/ turns silence into song." These are often words that spring up from the deepest part of experience, words that evoke those feelings, memories, and thoughts that cannot be articulated in literal terms but simply must be sung, a "concert in the flesh and bone." With his musician's ear, Van Slambrouck brings us echoes of those diaphanous feelings that exist even in the silences between the words. Poetry is the perfect form for his thoughts because it combines sound and image in a way that is as close to song as one can get, while still using language.

This book is a concert, suggested by the chapter titles: *Bass, Clarinet, Drums, Guitar, Piano, Saxophone, Trombone, Trumpet, Vibraphone,* and *Vocalist.* The poems sing often of his love for family in pieces like "My Father Was Lifted" and "Grandchildren Heal Her Loss." They sing of social justice in pieces like "Rosa," "Black Jazz," and "Sinkholes and Tsunamis." His voice is also laced with irony and sardonic humor, in pieces like "Bird Battle" and "Shooting Father Time."

There is a wonderful sense of connecting dichotomies in *Heart Music* as well, especially in poems like "Dissonance of Our Wounds," where he says, "Like musicians using dissonance/to produce a song of elegant whole,/our God uses dissonance of wounds/to create bright wonders within our soul." This collection of poems travels the many opposite notes of ecstasy and grief and, connecting them in an "elegant whole," helps us to see "bright wonders." It is a work of revelation as well as transformation.

It was my pleasure to work with Ed on *Heart Music* and see it come to fruition with him. He has been an enthusiastic student in many of my writing workshops, and I've always admired his ability to turn his wisdom, kind spirit and humor into poetry. I'm honored that he chose me to share in the creative process and help bring his works to the world in this beautiful book. He is a man of great dedication to his art who has a gift for hearing reverent music in a complicated world. He has truly created a symphony of the soul that will bring many readers pleasure.

With gratitude and love,

Margo LaGattuta

BASS

There was the bass-player, wiry redhead
with wild eyes, jabbing his hips at the fiddle
with every driving slap, at hot moments his
mouth hanging open trancelike.

From "On the Road"
by Jack Kerouac

Heart Music*

A concert in the music of the heart
turns hot to cool; the golden tone
booms in the treble tomb.
Music in the chamber of the veins
turns silence into song; blood in the sounds
brings up the living worm.

A concert of the ear forewarns
bones of tone deafness, and the womb
works in a death as life pumps out.

A silence in the concert of the ear
is half its sound; the tone and pitch
pounds on spherical shore.
Seed that makes notes deep in the loin
rings half its fruit, and half drops down
slowly with a quiet woodwind air.

A concert in the flesh and bone
is soft and loud; the quick and dead
perform like two horns for the ear.

A concert in the music of the world
plays horn with drum; each mothered child
lies within the double bass.
A concert blows the moon's salient sounds,
turns over last folds of the score,
and the heart gives its last throb.

*This parallel poem follows the form of Dylan Thomas'
A Process in the Weather of the Heart.

Jazz Trio and Guest

… I listened to his speedy, mellow alto
pouring out of two big maples as if West
Coast jazz were the music of Nature itself.
From "Jazz and Nature" by Billy Collins

Black, white and tan
keys tingle and tickle the ear
when fingertips trip
scale after scale of transient tones
forcing feet to beat and
hearts to pump happiness
into lives living in music.

Bass plucked sounds radiate
waves of wide vibrations
causing humming and heads
nodding to tunes that tune
the mind to emit streams
of endorphins that rain,
splashing musical colors.

Drum rims crack and snap
setting the tempo that drives
notes into the soul.
Socks bop the bass pulse
with pace that coalesces
the trio and underscores
melodic improvisation.

A single string of swirling sax sounds
graces the whole toward audio
pleasure that pleases the trio
and perks their inventive prowess
producing variations that
twist through three octaves
of musical paint, creating jazz.

Birds Flock

Screeching caw of the gull
penetrates our condo wall.
Graceful pesky fowl swoops down,
begs with caustic call.

Ancient pelicans with bulging
beaks float by my window to seek
nesting respite on an isle of teeming life,
full of bird droppings covering their feet.

Groups of rare white pelicans swim
to circle food with working feet.
Teams of twenty set the table
to eat with cooperative beat.

Wide-winged great egret, elegant
with green mask about the eyes
glides to land and rise again through
mangrove trees with loud cries.

Would a wood stork bring us baby trees?
Lazy bird stands still on one stilt.
Beady eyes dart on turkey brow, her
black-ended wings stretch to the hilt.

Pink feathers color the absurd roseate
spoonbill mud connoisseur.
Perhaps this platypus-billed bird
is a flaw of Mother Nature.

Black cormorant stands on a post
looking like a German banner top.
Chasing fish under water is fun
for this double-crested water cop.

The long, down-curve billed ibis
probes muddy beach for a tasty treat.
Her wings beat at a brisk pace;
then they glide without a beat.

A stately great blue heron stands tall,
head erect waiting to pierce with spear.
Rookery nests are towering forts
where snakes and cats would tread with fear.

The osprey soars over coasts,
eagle-like, searching for food
for his brood who nest in a dead tree.
They are in a hungry mood.

Some Florida birds look absurd,
yet all give pleasure to the eye.
When snow-birds see them soaring,
they think, *Soon I'll rise in the sky.*

What I Am, I Am

I'm a bowl of Cheerios with slices
of yellow banana. I might be a plate of
Eggbeaters, sometimes an English
muffin with strawberry jam on top.
Without a couple of cups of coffee
I'm never really what I am.

I'm what's left to nuke when the fridge
has gifts to give. If not that, then two slices
of brown bread with cheese and ham,
lettuce and onion, mayo and mustard,
plus green olives and a pickle.
I'm cranberry-grape juice
or Pepsi, no caffeine, no sugar,
just bubbles. Sometimes, I'm a bottle
of beer or just H2O.

I'm a large plate of small noodle spaghetti.
The sauce, the sauce, oh what good taste I am.
Some days I'm chicken cacciatore on rice,
some days white fish soaked in vin blanc.
I'm definitely a dry chardonnay in a long-
stemmed glass, rarely a red beefsteak.
More often, I'm pasta with shrimp. On
special days, I'm raspberry cappuccino.

I'm an evening snack of healthy ice cream:
fudge royal, butter pecan, chocolate ripple
or perhaps plain vanilla with frangelico.
Since I'm so good, I'm a cookie, too.

The Student

I hustle across campus in April,
thinking about coeds, not metaphors.
I'm a mouse going to a hawk's nest
to sit with my bad habits and grades.

Passing a saucy gal on the quad
reinforces thoughts of females,
washes out thoughts of similes.
The hawk lands on his nest.

Settling in a back row in Poetry 101,
I note that girls outnumber boys, which
is why I'm not in Business 101.
The professor's nose is a hawk's beak.

The assignment to write a poem
with metaphors and similes is in
my three-ring-circus folder, ready
for that hawk's shredding.

Hawk hands back the test papers.
My extremities feel strange—
bleeding and torn-up. Is that
flesh there on my paper?

The Short Life of Misty

Caging a youngster may seen cruel,
inhumane—makes you feel like a warden.
But these young pups need to be taught
some lessons of life, some rules of living.
When a paw fells a dirt plant,
when a food mess messes the kitchen,
when clothes get spread through the house,
then the hammer must nail the offender.

My line of children play kindly with her
and she with them, erasing all doubt
that she has any meanness in her soul.
A grandchild's long flowing hair blends with
Misty's hair—reddish, nearly like a radish.
Her long nose nuzzles our little ones
during play-filled summer days.

Then there are the wars:
possum, raccoon and skunk.
Misty's a teen and nothing
can enter our territory. She repels
foreigners promptly.
Most of Misty's battles are standoffs
except one defeat from the rear
guard of a white striped warrior.
It ends in a bloody catsup bath.

Misty receives full membership in our clan.
She is loved, scolded, played-with,
coddled and cuddled by family in a way
that is tough and tender, fun and full of life.
A hairy, panting, wet-nosed,
happy-to-meet-you-at-the-door canine
enhances life, reduces stress.

The jaws of death blind-side us all.
The lump on her upper left jaw
grows fast with flesh-eating tentacles
boring into bone and spirit.
The vet, cutting to dispatch
the evil growth, fails.
A darker, deeper cancer
covers Misty's mouth.
She no longer eats,
no longer romps and she
gazes with Picasso eyes
into our eyes, asking *why?*

At the Humane Society
our golden dog looks with
asking eyes, while "Fatal Plus"
enters her vein. Eight years of
Misty's love erase her year of pain.

Driving home, I retrieve
from a cluttered mind
an Earl Garner line:
*I'm too misty and
too much in love.*

Reflections on a Solar Kiss

Blinding orb of light, a circle
of searing thermonuclear
fire, is hot as freezing sickle
of raw ice, crystal clear.

We sit on canvas chairs
placed on beach shore edge.
My lover covers our legs
with a blanket of warmth.

Reflective ray of orange-yellow,
interrupts a line of sand, beams
low across the Gulf of Mexico,
shows the flow of the color band.

We watch bird flocks search for
bits of food on the sandy water way
and carefree youths hunt tiny shells.
She leans over; we share a kiss this day.

Tennis and Beer

A player should know the serve is key
to a success-filled day. One should
prefer clever placement inside
white borders. Don't you agree?

Power stroking with the forehand
is not foreplay for mixed doubles.
It seals set points for wins,
turns foe into lame lamb.

A smooth backhand, flowing with juice
provides added points easy on joints.
Jerky movements are mental
backs-of-the-hand causing the deuce.

Hitting the ball back is my best
scoring finesse, my strategy.
The lob, the drop, the smash and more
sit in my bag unused. No jest.

Oh, to have a clean win—the goal!
At match end, I search my soul
and hurt as I sit on my tailend
wishing to crawl into a hole.

Then life becomes refreshed with cheer,
banter and beer. After two Buds,
partners and foes tell jokes and laugh.
So screw unforced errors. More beer?

The Golden Moon

The new reed on my saxophone gives me
trouble, some squeaks, like those in life.

Moonlight, Moonglow, Moon Rays, Moon Love:
These old ballads can swing; they're cool and warm.

When I was really young, I danced with my dream girl
to the sweet melody of *Moonlight in Vermont*.

I programmed computers for the moon rocket
named *Saturn*. Both bodies are not green cheese.

I viewed moon rocks once, looking for a glow
within those gray chunks, hoping for something more.

During my divorce, the moon was covered
by earth's shadow, along with my dark shadow.

We hope for fulfillment and seek love.
For diversion, I riffed on moonless nights.

My blue moon-mood broke when Diane
arrived to bring harmony to my life.

My Yamaha shines like gold and silver.
My hair once golden is moon-silver now.

The keys on my sax, pushed for highs and lows,
create sounds much like tides from the moon.

Lend Me Your Ears

Lend me your ears not your eyes
to sense the glory of color-filled art.
Hear musical tones deep in paint.
Art turns sight into sound for ears.

Sensing the glory of color-filled art
injects the soul with creative glee.
Art turns sight into sound for ears.
Poetic metaphors for eyes to hear

inject our soul with creative glee.
The Bard writes of Anthony—
poetic metaphors for eyes to hear.
Van Gogh, less one ear, applies color.

The Bard writes of Anthony,
lend me your ears, not your eyes.
Van Gogh, less one ear, applies paint,
hears musical tones deep in paint.

Hubbard Glacier

HISSSS, CRACK, SWOOSH, SPLASH!
We huddle together to view slices
of sliding ice in random rhythm
that melt in the gray water
and flow from bay to ocean way.

HISSSS, CRACK, SWOOSH, SPLASH!
More blue ice is exposed by calving.
Another wave to bob the slabs of ice.
Where these ancients split from the womb
becomes a toss in a game of dice.

Massive ice river falls broken
with cries of anguish and shouts
of cannon during its wet demise.
HISSSS, CRACK, SWOOSH, SPLASH!
Wow, that one was a whopper!

Wind wails, rain drops, mist fogs
the decks where we cruisers crane
our necks to feel the sound
of mammoth ice-wall wham.
HISSSS, CRACK, SWOOSH, SPLASH!

Our ears are bitten by wind and moans of freedom.
Our eyes reflect white and blue then turn to red.
Our teeth chatter while our minds are numb
with visions breaking off edges of ages.
HISSSS, CRACK, SWOOSH, SPLASH!

Toes and noses near frozen
decree the need to flee the deck.
We go back to stateroom warmth
to leave old ice in its final trek.
hissss, crack, swoosh, splash.

Dancing in the Dark

In 1948, Dad convinces Mom
to pull up Michigan roots and stake
a claim in sunny, healthy Arizona.

Fresh out of high school,
I don't favor this trip to
another life in cowboy land.

Dad, Mom and we three board
a small house-trailer and head
on a tour of the new wild west.

After two months of seeing
ranges, with and without mountains,
we arrive at the edge of Phoenix.

This bird, in the hot sands of native
Indian lands, welcomes white easterners
who have resources to burn.

Dad sells the house-trailer and buys
a grocery store, renaming it Van's Foods.
They say the business will grow
while homes replace desert cactus.

The experiment fails the next year.
A recession, in white man's land, kills
the dream hard work tried to repair.
The year hands us a harsh lesson with
that paradise-to-be leaving its mark on me.

One dandy dent to my psyche
occurs on a trip to the Grand Canyon.
We stay two days and a night near
the south rim of that majestic abyss.
The sky-blue-wide, to the other side,
amazes us with its transparent air.
The sun renders ridges of rainbows.

On the first night, fortune smiles on us.
A group of red men from a local
reservation dance the Spirit
Dance near the south rim;
they whoop loud around a
crackling fire, which itself
dances with flickers of flames—
men and fire make ghostly
shapes, dark and fierce.

It's a cool, windy night with no moon.
I taste dust from deerskin feet,
hear the multiple tom-tom beat.
Burning bark wafts into my nose.

Barebacked braves move past me
while wailing songs of lament.
Goose bumps lift on my body
during this long, spirit-filled dance.

I have a twitch of fear watching
those gyrating shadows. Am I
seeing the ghosts of Wounded Knee?

CLARINET

… and go cool-quiet and waked the blues,
listen listen and the light come through.

From "The Clarinet"
by Sean Singer

Freedom in Jazz

Feel the rhythms of heart and soul,
deep in mostly steady beat.
Hear   the   base   and   drum
which   put   the   tem   po
to   the   hot   cool tune
play   ing   in   ron   do.

Guitar and piano play chords
that augment and key the band.
They pick solos and design arpeggios
while the big round sounds come
from sharp snare and string base.
Catch the melody, crisp and cool,
from bold brass and wailing rich reed.
The saxophone sings its song,
                    blowing
          our ears.   triplets
                around

                              high notes.
                reaches for
The trumpet
The trombone
                probes for
                              low notes.

The chart flows through a grace land
of blues, then bright oranges and reds.
Care and joy occur in smiling harmony
from both clefs' string of pearly notes.
Innovation breathes with improvisation,
firing from all sides in ordered discord.
With steamy syncopation, drumbeats
harmonize musician and fan.

Doubt

I doubt that is thrown at me
when I argue the cons of politics
with conservative cats of prey,
who drone on to give me eye tics.

Doubting, it seems, is in vogue.
The market, our health and world news
gang up on our attitude toward life
to give us palpitations and the blues.

I reach for the counterpoint of jazz:
its joyous beats charm my mind
much like being in bed with Diane
listening to her breathe in like kind.

To limit doubt, we go to church
to hear the Word. Father Joe can do
homilies of honey. He's cool,
has us loving Muslim and Jew.

To my dismay, Joe preaches on doubt,
saying his family gives him support
to limit his pain and calm his brain.
He claims this gives him comfort.

On the drive home, we chat about Joe's
talk. I wonder out loud, *Why did he
go on about doubt?* Diane replies,
He didn't say doubt; he said gout.

The Hunchback

He is short, hunchbacked.
Some call him dwarf.
He tends Mr. Leather's gardens,
does handyman stuff for that rich guy.
His main job is keeping kids out
of his master's cherry trees.

Mulberries are tasty,
but those black bing cherries
win our gang's taste test.
We fear getting caught
by that hunchback dwarf,
but fear doesn't hinder our taste
for bravery or bragging rights.

Floyd and I have a plan for a feast:
Visit at lunch time, climb high, eat our fill
and wait until we see no human sign.
Then climb down and run like hell.

At 2 PM, Hunchback strolls toward us
with hoe in hand. He calmly looks up at us
and yells, *You two get down here*!
We think, *Up yours; no way.*

He threatens cops, a call to our parents
and legal action by the rich guy.
We start to worry. The hoe looks like an ax.
The dwarf seems to get taller.
My friend starts to cry, as we
climb down with bellies full of cherries.

Before Hunchback can grab us,
we hightail it home to wait for the phone call
which never comes,
except in my repeating dream.

Rocks

pulled to the edge of the woods
by a team of mules
harnessed to a sled,
a century and a half ago,
allowed farmers freedom
of land use, freedom to bear fruit
and gave me license to cuss.

Our backyard garden rocks
deposited at lot's edge
cleared fields for crops or cows
that fed families of nine or more,
provided an ownership line
and forced hard labor onto me.

Coats of leaves each year
hid the rocks like land mines
that, when struck by a shovel,
damaged my back, legs and arms.
What were they thinking
those dead cultivators?
No time to build a rock wall?

Now flowers flourish among
those Alcatrazian rocks.
A biological rainbow covers
that old rocky spine,
that prismatic line
at the woods' edge,
where once I dredged.

Looking for Love

We cry right out of the womb
from a slap that greets a new guest.
Safely, we rest on the comfort
of our mother's warm breast.

We cry when we skin a knee
on a tricycle, falling on our rear.
Love pours onto a Band-Aid
to heal our tot-hood fear.

We cry obliquely at puberty
with feelings that alter the mind.
Assurances, unsaid by parents,
dispense love of a different kind.

We cry with joy at our wedding
for the togetherness of love
when we toast our guests and
watch them release the white dove.

We cry for our children when
elbows are bruised, loves leave,
grades are unfair or jobs are lost.
When children are ill, we grieve.

We cry at family events
be they joyful or tragic strife.
All contacts are acts of love,
even when we down-size life.

We cry out in prayer during
our last hour to allay fear.
God, please love and care for
us within your infinite sphere.

Sand and Water

Shell Island lies across green-blue water.
Markers and buoys stand near sandbars
warning kayaks, canoes and jet skiers
who make trails of white foam on the water.

A plethora of feathered flocks
wait on shallow bars, look
for finned fish scooting in the water.

A no-named thin peninsula juts into
the green-blue ending with white sand
where pipers trod in the water.

Waves lap near the shore where
I sit waiting for friends to return from
strolling the beach through waves of water.

I'm told they happen upon a huge
sand sculpture of a sea turtle,
art that awed them near the water.

Next time someone else
can watch the darn picnic gear,
which sits near the churning water.

Phonetic Alphabet Application

I sometimes envy the *alpha* dog
that dominates his domain
demanding cheers of *bravo*
from friends or foes who dummy-up
to the likes of *Charlie* Mc Carthy.

With their pomposity,
they flood the *Delta* during
Katrina. The damage *echoes*
around our country even to where
fox trot on the hills of Kentucky.

They play *golf* on a resort
hotel course, chat and laugh
about cheap labor in *India*
that affords them mistresses
named *Juliett*, Roseline or Livia.

I sometimes wish to be thousands
of *kilo*meters away from thoughts
of hate, perhaps to *Lima*, Peru,
to hear ancient culture chatter
from a guide named *Mike*,

which is the name of my son
who lives in Tennessee.
Each *November* we visit
and eat veal *Oscar* dinners.
(His son, Mikey, has a fine *papa*.)

Or I could travel to *Quebec*,
where massaged French is spoken
by local *Romeos*, to deter
thoughts of hunger and flies in the lives
of children of the *Sierra*,

or I could go to arty Paris,
not to do a last *tango*,
see the *uniforms* of the Iraq war
or hear the false
claims of a *victor*.

Instead, I'll have a *whisky* to forget
what my last *Xray* shows,
be content with my *yankee* home
and read about the *Zulu*
in the *Smithsonian*.

Preamble to a Jazz Orchestra

*Take off your skin and dance in your bones**

Big band music is born in Dixieland,
but Dixie isn't played in sweet tea gardens.
What forces Fletcher and King to reign?
How do Fats and Jelly Roll play that swell?
Why do we flock to hear Duke and Benny?

*Put out your can, here comes the garbage man**

Swing dances in with glitter and jitter.
Dorsey renews the bones.
Thornhill makes new chords moan.
Miller's a filler when he's in the mood.
Brown is sentimental.
Hampton is never tame.
Basie booms one more time.
Ellington's tunes gain great fame.

*Oop bop sh' bam, a klook a mop**

Bebop blows higher than the moon.
Parker parks on top of that moon.
Krupa drives with booming beats.
Kenton arranges harsh balanced feats.
Herman fields his herd of cats.
Gillespie's bent horn bends our ears.
Raeburn creates without beers.

*Hit that jive, Jack; put it in your pocket till I get back**

In the last half of the past century
big jazz bands ware hidden somewhere.
Stan designs bright bands.
Woody has four hip bands.
Boyd retires early to the Smithsonian.
Diz goes Cuban and blows a blast.
Gene drives coast-to-coast much too fast.
The Bird lives on and on, for bop is his.

*It don't mean a thing if it ain't got that swing**

Bigness survives behind the rocks.
Rob Mc Connell had a damn fine sound.
Thad Jones flourishes with tunes abound.
Buddy Rich's sticks are a bitch.
Louis Bellson is more than bold.
Maynard Ferguson blows at a high pitch.
McCoy Tyner doesn't fold, I'm told.

*The 21st century brings added innovation, more big
bands and seminal jazz music to play at any gig.*

*These lines are taken from tunes by various jazz
instrumental groups that performed during the
twentieth century.

Naked Art

Inside the Palacio De Bellas Artes
hangs Diego Rivera's art on red marble
walls. He hangs everywhere there. Leaving
the Latino artist to his wall fame
we wander on this sunny day
the museum's field of white marble.
Youthful lovers hug near museum corners, while
businessmen march quickly past
open-air naked marble statues.

Suddenly, the sound of odd-timbered
drums comes from the street corner, where
traffic flows like schools of fish. Our
eyes widen with the view of 300
copper-skinned Mexicans disrobing.

The men place placard pictures of a
politico over their bronze genitals, while
women, with their golden skin, hold
flyers in one hand and a donation can
in the other. Their dark bushes and round
brown breasts are free to see.

This first day in Mexico City is a big
hit. We smile wide and we hear ourselves
laugh. Three naked ladies ask us for pesos.
When two more come our way,
we retreat to the hotel.

During the three block stroll,
we joke and pun gratitude with
Muchas gracias, senor con senora.
I think, on the elevator, if Rivera
were alive, he would be out there
with canvas and brush, painting
like hell those placards and bushes.

Rosa

Near the dome of the state capital
lies a polished black stone table
in front of a black granite wall,
where Martin's stalwart words reside.
Upon the pedestal rests Maya Lin's
tabletop, exact, its perimeter incised
with civil rights fact after fact:

November 13, 1956: the Supreme Court banned
segregated seating on Montgomery buses.
Rosa's action was validated. I
walk around that tabletop
in warm Alabama sun, see
its calm water roll slowly down.

Her humble soul took a stand,
yeah, took a seat for liberty. This
soft black icon gives hope
to our diverse society. Now we
wait in Rosa's line, we whites
embrace for hours black brothers and
sisters whose hearts pump red as ours.

The stream of mostly black skin
flows slowly toward Rosa's *au revoir*,
like the water flowing down the sides
of that stone altar. The wait purifies our
souls, allows our hearts to see free.
We walk a slow steady march by
Rosa's white-laced bed, solemnly.

Rosa lived Martin's words. She
sat for freedom: The call of those
words fixed on that nine-foot tall wall:
… until justice rolls down like waters
and righteousness like a mighty stream.

Siblings

The black and white photo of my First
Communion in 1938 has we three
standing to face a Kodak Brownie.
Mom snaps a moment in infinity, which
proves I part my hair on the right.

I'm eight wearing polished new shoes,
knickers that bulge at my knees,
white tie melting into white shirt.
My hands impede my two-year-old
brother with a touch of love,
holding him from worldly evils.

My haircut is bowl-like, showing strong
ears, dark eyes and a hint of a smile.
Paul stands between our sister and me.
There is no escape from the toddler trap.
His small high-top shoes are ready
to run at the sound of a shutter.

Mary Ann, age 5, holds Paul's right
hand tightly. A Mickey Mouse watch
encircles her wrist. She protects
her curly-headed baby brother
with the sureness of kindled love.

Her blond hair, with a wide red ribbon,
augments her checkered dress with
its white collar and sleeves. Her shoes
are pure white, as opposed to my sheer
black. Her sweet face is full of future.

We three stand aside the vined back porch
with its wrinkled wood steps, lined with irises.
Our eyes speak of where we will go.

Smithery

The smithy works with his anvil,
shaping and reshaping metal,
working with purpose to gain perfection.

The wordsmith creates moods and attitudes
with word paintings using colors and shades,
bending words into subtle nuances.

The poet's tools of rhythm, rhyme
and meter hammer and hone lines
into streams of sparks.

Raw materials gleaned from life
shape aesthetic ideas,
send soft signals to you, the reader.

DRUMS

... the fixed grin joins the menacing stare,
especially suitable for long drum solos.

From "The Many Faces of Jazz"
by Billy Collins

Black Jazz

Before Bull Conner's dog days,
a Birmingham, Alabama hotel
quarters three soldiers in transit
through that red clay state.
In the South in '54, white is right.

Bored, I take an evening walk
in that black city to breathe free air.
Distant jazz drifts into my mind,
which forces my ear to hear more
and my pace to seek the source.

The second floor dance floor is
a black sea of laughter and cool
jazz. The big-busted black lady
does not sell me a ticket, saying,
You take care, ya hear?

The alley next to the dance hall
holds two young men, dark as
shadows, digging the jazzy tunes.
Joined together, our pairs of ears
groove on the spectrum of bebop.

A cop walks by the alley's mouth,
then reappears surprised.
What you doin' here white boy?
Explaining the need for jazz, I'm
met with a raised nightstick.
Okay, okay, I'm leaving. Sorry.

Cancun

Blackbirds dip beaks in the pool
to refresh their throats,
then hop to the shallow end
to bathe their glossy feathers.
Mariachi fills the air.

Cancun, Cancun, Cancun.
Cool breeze, music, hot tune.

Troughs direct water to fall
into two pools. Green tiles
change the clear to turquoise
mimicking the emerald sea
that laps the blistering beach.

Cancun, Cancun, Cancun.
We love your sun and moon.

This last day of our tour
brings music of respite:
the lift of margaritas,
the boarding pass to Detroit,
the feeling of fun well done.

Cancun, Cancun, Cancun.
Back to the grind too soon.

Carpenter Tools

Our roots become trees as our seeds transfer.
He worked wood and leather with tools made by hand.
My hands become my grandfather's.

He repaired my mother's shoes with his tack hammer.
His level eyeballed hearth, doorjamb and night stand.
Our roots become trees as our seeds transfer.

Using these tools, I hang kin on tacks to confer
roots for my children. What guides my right hand?
My hands become my grandfather's.

My level, honed and held by that carpenter,
is made out of a yard of pine, has no brand.
Our roots become trees as our seeds transfer.

Building a paver patio by the pond, I prefer
to drift in mind, to think how he leveled the land.
My hands become my grandfather's.

I hold his worn level, smooth without spur.
I use his hammer, balanced and grand.
Our roots become trees as our seeds transfer.
My hands become my grandfather's.

Cutting the Lawn

Ben finds three engine mount bolts
broken off my John Deere mower.
It's good to have a mechanic
as a handy-boy grandson.

After two weeks, the mower is healed,
but the grass is high as a squirrel's eye
and populated with frogs. I mount my
mower to trim around the lawn's ears.

On the first pass, frogs and toads
hop away when they hear a
monster mower coming their way.

On the third pass, I run over a
snake, clip the tip of his tail.
Checking him, I see a deep wound
across his belly gaping at the sun. Mr.
Deere cut him to an irreparable state.

On the sixth pass, I checked him
again and still see life.
Picking up the slinky carcass,
I carry it into the woods
behind our house, lay it near
a century old apple tree.

The next day I go to see
the snake and bury him,
giving him proper rites, but he's gone.
Was he a meal for a woods critter,
a toy for the neighbor's dog?
Was he bestowed new life
by a distant relative who once
wrapped himself around
another apple tree for Eve?

Artichoke Snack

We assemble for an afternoon snack,
a gourmet course. After a pause, Chef
Kurt displays raw buds of artichoke.
The reaction is much applause.

Artichoke sweetmeat is well known.
This veggie, of the thistle tribe
of Mediterranean lineage, is prime.
These California buds thrive in sun.

Chef Kurt puts a dozen in a pot
with salt, oil, bay leaf and a magic pinch,
boils this pleasant brew a lot,
coaxes sweet flavor with a

bowl of garlic butter at each place,
a colorful napkin at each plate.
He sets condiments for the odd taste,
places pot buds on a steel slate.

One by one, each bud sheds its bracts.
We start to slurp with each leaf-like bract,
dip leaves and then scrape with our teeth.
Near the heart, the flesh is sweet.

Di and Ed in Palindromes

Wow, I say when my eye,
radar tuned, scopes the sexes.
Level and sure, I spot a pip.
Aha, I think you were a nun.
(God is kind for this old dog.)

Madam, I say, *We are not deified.*
Civic need and physical deed
pop up at odd times, so don't nod.
You are top-spot on my list for a gig.
Ed gives love a toot for Di's id.

Dissonance of Our Wounds

Our wounds bleed from broken relationships,
illness, injury, crime and tragedy.
Some wounds result from our mistakes.
Some may still bleed with controlled ease.

Most over time have healed,
and scars are the aftermath.
Scars are a part of our lives,
staying even after death.

After death, all scars transform,
no longer show our darker side.
They shine forth in transcendental form
when we join our wounds with Christ.

Like musicians using dissonance
to produce a song of elegant whole,
our God uses dissonance of wounds
to create bright wonders within our soul.

Decision for Dad

Why did I insist Dad get that pint of blood?
Oh yes, he told me by nodding yes
which shook the tubes around his head.
It's pointless to waste blood, the doctor said,
since Dad was failing on that death bed.
I ordered the blood into his vein.
He lived three more months in pain.

A bus took Mom to where
Dad's machines were pumping.
He could not rise to accept her kiss
when each day she was at his side.
My brain faltered. How did I miss
her slipping to fragility
before that bloody decision?

Those months increased her senility,
drove seeds of dementia
deep into her sweet soul's calm
and guilt into me. I will
never forget that blood stain.

I plead to God that my loony
obedience didn't matter
though it amplified their pain
and created a conundrum that
today still beats in my heart,
the sad drumming of a blues tune.

By the Pond

The lad sits on the edge
of the pond world
looking at yellow water lilies
like a young Plato or Socrates.

Grasses tall along the waterfall,
small fir trees setting aside blooms
and boulders bold in their fixed stance
force the boy into a thinker's trance.

Slippery rainbow carp,
oblivious of frog and human,
swim lazily in their clear deep.
A dragonfly flies in a wide sweep.

The boy gets bored and
develops a supply of phlegm,
aims with careful wish
and spits twice at the fish.

Love's Slow Dying

Love's slow dying speaks of a life of light.
Embraced youth delights every sweet day.
My God, loss wounds me, tears in half my night.

Victor and Sandy's preemie son, born in strife
doubles their love, cloaking future essay.
Love's slow dying speaks of a life of light.

She holds my son's heart and hand tight,
even when her cancer foretells doomsday.
My God, loss wounds me, tears in half my night.

Christmas becomes dark and brings plight.
Sandy dying, will rise again, I pray.
Love's slow dying speaks of a life of light.

Ben stands small beside that gray gravesite.
Please, Daddy, let's go; I'm cold. Dismay!
My God, loss wounds me, tears in half my night.

Victor, my son, please look to your insight.
My love stays in life and in hard clay.
Love's slow dying speaks of a life of light.
My God, loss wounds me, tears in half my night.

Golf and Tennis

Dad likes cigars, cards, and golf.
Some badges of his personality are:
being an usher at St. Mary Church,
being a VP of the paper mill union,
having a good-time-Joe attitude.

Paul, my six-year-younger brother,
bonds with Dad like cement setting.
I love Dad but I think some of his
ventures float on frothy waves.

When Dad retires from the mill,
my love for him grows stronger,
not with super glue like Paul's
but glue nevertheless. Golf is one
of Dad's and Paul's tubes of glue.
They play every chance they can.
Dad's handicap is low for age 70.

Feeding six children, I have
no time or funds for golfing fun.
Tennis takes half the time and is
better exercise—my choice sport.

Dad asks to play tennis, so
I lend him my Wilson racket,
better than his old one—
wires strung for strings.
Surprise—he's playing pretty well.
We get wired, no strings attached.

I hit a hot one right at Dad's feet:
he back-peddles, trips and falls.
Spry for his age, Dad puts his hand
out behind him for a soft fall.

The doctor determines that Dad
broke his wrist. I'm shocked to see
his cast, which screws up his golf
for a year. I'm 100% repentant, 200%
apologetic and 300% miserable.
Dad and I apply a lot of cement
to our love-relationship.

GUITAR

… and when he played guitar would somehow hold the strings with crippled fingers.

From "Django Reinhardt"
by Peter McSloy

Jazz at the Cadieux Cafe

Aficionados of jazz
crave innovative sounds. We
amble into the corner café, where
mussels meet the nose, tight
tables adorn the old wood floor, and
rows of Belgium prints surprise our eyes.

On keyboard command,
musicians arrive at their stands.
The book is scanned and
the set is set with sheets of charts.
Hands adjust straps; horns warm up.

Gwinnell taps the tempo,
starting a funky Monk thing.
The band jells without a shirk.
Our heads nod and begin to jerk.
A calliope of sound flows into
our ears, moves around our
minds and ends in our souls.

There is a wealth of charts
in this band's cooking book.
Composers by the score:
Dave and Diz, Bill and Scott,
Woody, Quincy and Toshiko, too.
A Thad tune ends in Central Park.

Bands swing songs with horns and hands.
Saxophones wail and scale. Brass
reach high, some moan deep. Rhythm
beats with chords on strung strings.
The band crosses the bridge in
Chelsea at a fast pace. Audio-
joy shows on my face.

Five saxophones harmonize
with altos pairing while tenors tenderly bark
staccato undertones, then play solo riffs.
The bari belches like a bottom feeder.
Blues and greens flow inside majors and minors.
Kamiski's soprano is a saintly voice. Wood's
tenor is a whirlwind carnival of notes.

Three trumpet notes start the next set
with the sound of Perdido at its head.
Mark solos with his talking mute.
Flugelhorns mellow the melody
with scales of soft sound. Gabriel-like
tones mimic the bones. Trumpets
tear at our ears.

Tempo tightens with blaring trombones,
slide and valve pumping low moans.
Bass bone vibrates in unison with
bari and acoustic bass. Euphonium
argues with a tenor echoing
interlaced tones. The tuba's
timbre seems scuba-like,
dives deep into a sea sound. Resonating
trombones punctuate a mambo.

Rhythm units guide bands like
gardeners fostering their flowers.
Chords underline each measured meter.
A board of keys states structure, while
solos wiggle around with sound. Percussion
presents a presto bent with snare,
cymbal and bass beat. The drums
hum with pulsating bursts moving
the music by tempo and time. The band's
throbbing bass-heart thumps
while driving a Mingus piece.

The cafe becomes a dizzy-land of dissonance
with horns in wild fugue and rhythms rocking.
Sixteen men blow a rhapsody of melodies with
discord of harmonies producing pandemonium.
We are flown to the moon with stardust by starlight.
That old black magic pushes our feet to tap
with electric waves of audio thrills.

Infatuation

Limpid stars, I see no eyes.
Budding rose, I feel no lips.
There are no more little toys,
only your love, of dormant
progress. How I need to be
near your sensitiveness. I
dream of sweet sounds of a kiss.

I see eyes in a full-bloomed
rose and feel such a rush.
Laughter is yours and for your
happiness I long. Isn't mud
snow; isn't storm sunshine?
My wrung heart jars my mind
with lumps of questions.

A Spawned Poem

... the heart knows best that love and grieving
... keeps a steady iambic tally ...
                    from Thomas Lynch's poem
                    "Iambs for the Day of Burial"

Hearts beat their iambic pulse
for pleasure or fear
while exercising life,
which ends with the thud.
If we are lucky or good,
that exit will carry us yonder
to a seat next to God's
where we can discuss
the pros and cons of life.

What do you think about that guy
who raised his teenaged kids alone
when his wife flew the coop after one
and a half dozen years of marriage?

Well, he seemed to survive okay.

How about when that guy lost it
for over a year as he divorced
his wife and went into a funk,
some sort of a hate mode?

Too bad he wasn't frugal with his emotions.

Guess you're right, God, but what
would you do with such rejection?

Don't know—I've not been there, not done that,
yet lots of people have rejected me, too.

Grandbaby

Michael Andrew reminds
me of Christmas morning
when I was a small child.

Mikey's micro voice is the
sound of angel-like chimes.
His oval face is a merry-go-round
of music. His eyes, first blue
like sapphires, now hazel wide,
let me ride a roller coaster
of twinkling happiness.
Arms and legs, hands and feet
move like four tiny robots
covered by skin flamingo pink.

When proud parents touch
their son, there's a radiation
as warm as the sun. They are
living in their daily Christmas.

God's Love flows
when Mikey smiles.

Triskaidekaphobia as Applied to an Alstroemeria

1. Elephant Ears are poisonous, I'm told,
    and have no blossoms to cause fears.
    In counterpoint, this single yellow flower
    has tiny flecks of chocolate
    on each delicate petal.
    I'm tempted to eat it.

2. Flowers are for births, weddings,
    and deaths—the benchmarks of life.
    But this lily is a homework task
    assigned in a poetry class
    to numerically list visions,
    images and far-out thoughts
    of this ex-computer engineer.

3. This plant's sturdy pedical
    and clustered yellow top remind me
    of vast fields south of Paris
    where furlong upon furlong
    of sun flowers lean toward their namesake
    and ripple in the wind.

4. The lily's stem, long and thick, holds clusters
    of four leaves every two inches or so.
    I left four computer engineering jobs,
    during my work-for-money time.
    Leaves leave but return anew.

5. Lilies cover graves. Sandy had a blanket
    of lilies to rest under. Twenty-nine
    is too terribly young to die.
    Sandy was straight-up and full of trust.
    No hybrid Peruvian Lily was at her side,
    only pure white ones.

6. Each blossom has six yellow petals.
    I flowered six brightly colored children:
    Robin's-egg blue, warm mauve, bread brown,
    a field of violets, mint green and a ball of orange—
    hues of my love rainbow,
    the harmony of my seed.

7. Statistically, each stem has an average
    of 8.5 florets. Mine has 5.
    There was a time when I was short on joy
    and long on sorrow—
    about 3.5 lousy years.

8. Internet tells me this plant affords
    pharmaceutical products.
    Google says this plant can cause
    allergic dermatitis.
    Damn drug companies
    get ya coming and going.

9. An alstroemeria
    is the "Lily of the Incas."
    No wonder these plants are so resilient.
    Their ecological past
    was the ground of the Andes.

10. This weed with a top of gold is bugging me.
    I suppose the bees, dragon flies, humming birds
    and a plethora of insects groove
    on its flavors of favors. Ah nature,
    Mother or mistress, why do you tease us?

11. This growing pot of gold was named
    in honor of a Swedish diplomat.
    Our South American brothers forced
    the appended "meria."
    Europeans don't know
    how to herd llamas.

12. A cool number:
    a dozen roses,
    a dozen ears of sweet corn,
    cheaper by the dozen,
    a baker's dozen,
    twelve disciples,
    two six packs of beer,
    and a dozen alstroemerias.

14. Elevators do not have a button
    for floor 13 because hotels
    don't have that floor.
    I'm pretty sure I'm OK with 13
    but just in case,
    I omit this first teen,
    that puberty year.

The Monkeys of Palenque

The deep-jungle, hacienda-hotel
borders a dark gorge, where
deep-down lies a spa. We walk
down through sheets of vines,
thick-trunk trees and the smell
of monkey fecal matter.

Long furry-tails flick through the shadows
of the tallest trees. Harsh howls
at high decibels permeate
our ears at a tempo wild and woody.
Territorial beasts, projecting their best
New Year's party-sounds, try to generate
Mexican-jungle fear in us gringos.

After ten days of garlic pills and no bananas
to fortify our systems against mosquito attacks,
we find monkeys are the threat. Deeper
we go. Dusk is near. High-wire acrobats
demand that we leave.

We traverse the last stone steps
to arrive at the spa—outdoor mud bath,
steam room and massage table.
Then they attack. They're big, deadly,
and use mean weapons—
their noses full of malaria.

Waiting in the Casino

I try to take the sin out of
casino as I sit near the exit door
reading Billy Collins' *Sailing
Alone around the Room.*

This not-so-great hall room
has fifty to sixty multi-sized
not-so-cultural Indian artworks
symbolizing tribes, spirits,
earth, wind, water and fire
placed randomly about the walls.

The dichotomy presents itself
throughout the hall: ace of spaces,
wheel of misfortune, the wall's
base of stone that hints
of mother earth, a glass cabinet
of native artifacts, the constant
ring of slot machines.

A totem stands alone by the door,
urging old youngsters to bet more.
Buck antlers hanging there stare
down upon those who spend
coin but not one Indianhead penny.

All three kin are back. Two
faces smile wide. One face
has a lack of grin; he seems
empty inside like his wallet.

I will never see a casino tree.
God doesn't make money,
only delicious honey.

The Hampton House of Jazz *

Jazz lives with sounds of innovation, Gillespie-like,
and the Hampton legacy works in a metallic house
and, like Gillespie innovation, works in metallic sounds.

Valerie fingers flowers of sound, and
Marcus makes the audio harmonious.
The alto saxophone matches a tone
to warm lips on the flugelhorn.
Lips and fingers on the alto saxophone
make Valerie's sound warm.
Marcus matches harmonious tone of the
flugelhorn to the audio flowers.

The drumbeat makes heads go up and down.
Feet tap to notes fast, tight and loud.
Drumheads tight—to beat feet fast.
Notes go up and down and make the tap loud.

The house of Marcus Hampton lives to tap feet and
the drum makes heads go up and down to the beat.
The flugelhorn matches notes with like sound, loud, tight.
Innovation, warm lips and fast fingers make
harmonious sounds in tone on the metallic alto saxophone.
Valerie Gillespie works a jazz legacy of audio flowers.

* Using the Billy Collin's Paradelle form,
modified for tongue-in-cheek efficiency.

Waves

The massive oil tanker cuts the
channel with a twenty-foot frontal
froth indicating a high-energy push.
The ship labors toward the harbor
bridge supported by its wire sails.

While we sit on a sunny beach bench,
the ship's waves, not perceivable
fifty yards away, noisily slap the wet
sand, distributing excess energy
the snorting sea monster makes.

On the other side of the globe,
a monstrous rip under the ocean
of India gives birth to death.
Hidden energy speeds in circles
toward lands teeming with people.

They are strolling the beach, laughing
at jokes. A tsunami wave, ready to wash
lives away, is undetected by technology
or tourists smiling at the shore's beauty,
unaware of the quake wake to come.

Death and beauty, hand in hand,
are no longer strangers. The
wave slithers back to the sea,
then brown bodies are placed
in Mother Earth's sandy graves.

Too Cocky

His bout in Toledo excites him. He's
geeked and ready for three rounds of
amateur boxing, using beet-red gloves. He
feels golden during his one-and-only fight.

Dad brags about that day of Golden
Gloves glory in 1921. That happens
when he listens on the old cabinet radio
to Billy Conn or the Brown Bomber
who's punishing some want-to-be.

Dad gives me fatherly advice:
Don't hitchhike, you're too young.
At 16, I'm a bit too cocky. Hell,
I'm playing my third year of football,
have muscles made of steel-rods.
Dad and I disagree about my prowess.

Our argument is put on hold,
since I have a gig playing
second-chair tenor sax in a big
band at a high school sox-hop.

The next day, Dad and I
again discuss hitchhiking.
We agree to settle the
dispute the honorable way.

Dad is golden, knocks me
down four times. I lose count but
get my licks in. Every time he pops
my head, I pop his body. The fight lasts
30 minutes and, exhausted, we quit.

The next day I come home
after football practice, surprised
to find Dad home from work.
Mom says, *Be quiet, Dad is resting.*
The doctor said he broke two ribs.

Later, I emotionally tell Dad I'm
sorry. I feel sad and guilty
but also a bit cocky.

The Sky

striped in a splurge of color,
seen this winter evening
from my condo balcony,
bubbles up thoughts
of distance and time.

While birds hustle overhead
headed to the island
rookery for their respite,
I put down a book of poems
to capture the bubbles.

I measure distance in sadness.
No, just the need to hear, see, feel
and laugh with our grandchildren,
wishing their energy would
radiate south from Michigan.

I measure time in times:
how many days do I have
to love my loves and write
these poems to tell my loves
how strongly I do love them?

Diane breathes deep in sleep—
a nap before her birthday meal.
I'll wake her soon before the moon
reflects those rapturous rays
from that striped sunset.

Writing Poems

The poet weaves and bobs
through his field of words.
His contracted lines of
thought illuminate a sunset
beach. Then with silk, he
skips to letters from Mom
when, in the Marines, he
holds his ground on the black
sands of Iwo Jima.

The poet knows power
aids disruption and
corruption, recalls a sight
like Baghdad's children
tagged with ripped rags
and shrapnel wounds yet
to heal, while oil depots burn,
remove sun from the desert
of war with plumes
of warming evil.

The poet fears his tears
burn the reader's eyes,
so he switches to younger
days when he clutches a
rubber gun, targets a friend
crouching behind a mulberry
tree. The band hits the enemy
square on his red shirt.

The poet then bends his pen
to a higher truth: his seed
that sired life and gave back
small voices full of laughter.

PIANO

… and music awards honor Dave, a grand piano poet, who invents sound-streams of joy.

From "Brewing Jazz"
by Edward V. Van Slambrouck

Jazz Festival

Hart plaza in Detroit is a jazz mecca.
Anticipation pumps my heartbeat like
a Bellson sock. The time for jazz during
Labor Day weekend highlights gigs
that will please both my musical ears.

Saturday's Jobim project, full of Latin notes,
absent of Nozero's sax, strikes a heavy beat.
Sean Jones' horn reaches colorful highs playing
charts for bopping along with popping sounds.
Payton's paten tones augment gutsy scores.

Sunday's stages hold Chico, Jon Faddis and
DeFrancesco's infinite whole note, while the
circuitous wail of Blake's saxophone and Riggins'
snare beat with its fierce cracking sounds abounds.
Man, this tune could blow Coltrane off the charts.

Monday brings more musicians to the altar
of grace notes peppered in scores much like
Art would have played. Shahida sings her songs
with a voluptuous voice. Music poet, Hendricks,
sets the beat with a raspberry voice counting time.

The festival joy fades, yet the scene
charts a course toward a better beat with
Collins, Walden, Wood, Weed, Budson,
Keller, Roe and other local musicians.
All that jazz is foot-tapping musical poetry.

I think how jazz, regardless of skin tone,
brings us together to tap and laugh. I note that
young or senior, black or white, a community
melds to bask in the musical score
of tolerance. Jazz wraps us in happy hearts.

Jesus Groans, Buddha Sighs

Jesus groans,
when sad seeds become harbingers at Pearl.
Humankind unkindly forces wars with weeping
weapons that paint the waters of the harbor
the red of death. Hegemony's critical balance
pitches and yaws. Yamamoto's fear doesn't
inhibit future yens, which end with sin.

Buddha sighs
when a poison mushroom generates death rads.
A bomb bellows a flood of blood from Enola
Gay. One hundred thousand Japanese and nine
Americans die, while flesh melts into red rivers
and God's children weep. La May's choice
closes the book on war before more horror.

Peace is piloted into potent reconstruction,
as products pile high on shores to share.
Life breathes fresh, while flesh no longer bleeds.
How do Buddha and Jesus embrace?
We heal and past fasting becomes open feast.
Our blue gem is a ring that links us together.

Glass Day

A gray glass day sets down
on the trees beyond our yard.
After the warmth of a false spring,
the wooden world becomes
a tundra bent in icy swing.

Rain rains pure icy water to
fashion a layered blanket that
coats plants in translucent lace.
A year-old leaf left on a branch
is frozen in time and space.

On a broken wild-cherry tree
an old crow scans the woods
that glisten bright in the sun.
The forest freezer traps all food
and the crow knows no fun.

Rabbits dream in cold hutches, while
nests of leaves hold pairs of squirrels.
They shiver in their treetop igloos.
Together they melt their frigid fur
while waiting for spring's menus.

Blue jay, wren and robin
flitter over splintered trees
weary of the winter scene.
They pine for a taste of spring
and yearn for a blanket of green.

We see both beauty and the beast
in crystals that cling to trees.
They look barren, but new life
waits deep. Come, sweet spring,
flower us with your bees.

A Place for Lut

for Leonard Lutwack*

The big city is his true place,
although his childhood home
a short distance from a large park,
providing in all seasons play
and mischief in hidden places,
sticks deeper in his mind.

Near his youth-filled home,
Hog River flows through
the fields of a dairy farm
affording him a place
for nude swimming.
He and his friends paddle
while the faint odor of cow
droppings wafts overhead.

The river flows by Mark Twain's
home in Hartford, Connecticut.
Lut thinks that Mark Twain
would love to see them
sitting on their clothes
so they won't blow away.

*My mentor's demeanor has diminished,
but not his place in my heart.

Sarcophagus

As religious leaders, we consider it one of our
duties to encourage and to support all efforts
made to protect God's creation, and to
bequeath to future generations a world
in which they will be able to live.
Benedict XVI and Patriarch Bartholomew

It's an earthly sarcophagus, a high and wide
mound of waste, a bulging pox mark that
looks like Beelzebub's belly supine on
our land. And the world dumps trash.

Birds caw and fill their craws with refuse
of our deposits: bits of crackers caked
on paper, partly used cans of chemicals,
boxes of ribbed condoms, broken baby
carriages, torn Emerson poems.
And words are made garbage.

Fire emits from mounds with a sound of
sheer silence from the bowels of a culture
that buys only the newest kind. The guide
to live simply, that others may simply live,
disappears in burning methane mass.
And darkness covers light.

Where is our stewardship for earth and
future generations? We are elephants
dropping waste wherever we roam,
mounds of dung heaping a legacy of
doom through unjust convenience.

Prelude to Loss

The essential sadness is to go through
life without loving. But it would be almost
equally sad to go through life and leave
this world without ever telling those you
loved that you had loved them.
    John Powell, "Unconditional Love"

Sweet fruit need not be bitter
nor lost star emanate flicker
because lovers know. Should
trees tell tales of happy times
and black rose break and cry
aloud, *The hurt is felt, love.*
Then let love be an Amen
and tears salt with no flavor
because lovers know.

Now none can say he never
has loved or cared or cried.

Grandchildren Heal Her Loss

Grandchildren heal her loss for a while,
erasing the sadness, the gloom, the moan.
Our unborn child has a silent smile.

A childless second marriage causes a trial
that needs new births to cool the tone.
Grandchildren heal her loss for a while.

Time travels slowly during denial
until my brood breeds kin, skin and bone.
Our unborn child has a silent smile.

Soft kisses wipe away any bile;
tots in tubs nourish our happy zone.
Grandchildren heal her loss for a while.

Moans are no more. We bask in a style
of love and new life, blessed and not alone.
Our unborn child has a silent smile.

Years of wonder go into exile
as my children spawn their own.
Grandchildren heal her loss for a while.
Our unborn child has a silent smile.

High Stepping

Their knees rise high; their arms swing
in the air. Strutting, with capes flying and
hats two feet taller than their heads, drum
majors flaunt their stuff. This band of lads
and lasses, flashing helmets of shining
chrome, march line after line in purple clad
waves. Twenty some drummers drum with
thunderous thuds and cracks on skins.
Thirty some horns of shimmering brass
swing at a cocky pace. These proud
black and tan players, celebrating Martin's
birthday, parade to honor dreamers.

When horn and reed are put to mouth
they sound like crescendos in the Pines
of Rome, bursting blasts across Central
Avenue that ricochet off bank, hotel
and cafe wall. Decibels puncture our ears
with a calliope of color, impacting our brains
like the liftoff of a moon rocket. The woodwinds
are positioned far in the rear. They blow drowned
sounds since drum and brass rule the atmosphere.

Musicians, dancers, flag wavers
and tall bobbing hats move on down
the street, a caravan of musical delight.
The joy starts to fade along the cement
canyon. I run ahead to catch more highs
radiating from that strutathon.

Revisiting

I sit upstairs in the FROG room
(Furnished Room over Garage).
I bet you were never in a frog room.
My old computer is in this room
where your last poem resides.

Remember when I was a young lad,
I promised to buy you a fur coat?
Perhaps these words will cover you
in warmth of a son's constant love.

To have two birds with one poem,
I have looked again at your life
and have rewritten that last poem
I wrote about your garden of love.

Much of what I'm saying you have
heard before in voice and written word.
Nevertheless, I place new twists
in my earlier poem to quell my sadness:

In the Hills and Hollers of Tennessee

you play with butterflies and bumblebees,
fireflies and sewing bugs, sit with Dad
on an old bent tree trunk. You work on
those lines producing paper, belting bullets
and burping babies, making that hospital
nursery a blanket of love. Holding all those
babies, all those years—mercy me.

You watch we three grow to multiply
in love, tend the blue, orange, red,
yellow flowers of earth, cook blueberry
muffins, chicken, dumplings and johnny-
bread, live ninety years with cigars,
bowling, golf, children of all ages.

You sit again with Dad beside his bed
with his pain yours in a year of grief,
wait eight long years to be with him again.
Smile kind soul yonder and sip cool spring water
in that heavenly holler not quite in Tennessee.

Puppy Dogs and Dragons

Garden weeds proliferate if not hoed.
Young flowers, stressed by milkweed,
poison elephant ears, and spinning
dragon breath can't breathe without space
to grow, without freedom during life.
Unjust war rips my soul's garden,
tears truth from our soil.

Killing, in year after year, breaks
hearts, decapitates and brings
uncivil civility. Good deeds build
gardens of colorful flowers, not fields
of weeds. Unjust war rips my soul's
garden, tears truth from our soil.

Gardens of the world suffer.
The poor hunger, and children
die by friend who is foe. Dragons
disguised as puppy dogs do
deeds that destroy our flowers.
Unjust war rips my soul's garden,
tears the truth from our soil.

God is a part of everyone. When
we kill each other do we kill
a bit of God? Let's use wisdom,
dismiss dragons and end ineptness.
Unjust war rips my soul's garden,
tears truth from our soil.

Ole Blue Eyes Lied

A movie date on Main Street Americana
is the norm 17 years after I was born.
An early Tennessee Williams play
converted to celluloid is playing.
We walk through the village green
over the River Raisin bridge on a
soft summer afternoon, talking
stiffly and laughing with strain.
I dare to get balcony tickets
because we both know that's
where the necking is.
My coat of arms, shyness,
impedes any advance.
Near the final act, the god of love
takes hold of me. Gently
taking her hand and enclosing
our fingers, I become electrocuted
with a reciprocating shock. This
small town girl puts my head into a
swirl. She squeezes my hand with such
tender power that I become numb, nearly
dumb, and to this day cannot remember
how we return to her house.

College dates, catch as catch can,
with a diverse milieu of city girls,
decompose me. On the love
battlefield at 21, I am still a raw recruit,
but I get lucky. An athletic gal takes a
liking to me. Her cute figure enhances
her figure skating skills in my
amorous eyes. I talk of Arthur Miller's
new play while she smiles and chatters
about how high the lead male skater
can toss her during their routine.

The romance goes on in its mild way
without her perfumed hair coming undone.
I have no training, no skill in forging
hot bodies together with word or deed.
In two months the dream dries
with a short, lips-closed kiss.

After marriage come six hungry children.
A real wife is not a blue-blooded girl
with independent means
who drives around in limousines.
A real wife bleeds red
working with diapered babies
and children with runny noses.
She dreams and envies
her 35-year-old spouse
when he goes to the respite of work.
She employs herself with zeal
when cash doesn't flow.
A real wife and her man
have no time or temperament
to discuss Eugene O'Neill's
A Touch of the Poet.

The days grow short as we travel
toward the December of our years.
Autumn time is vintage, sweet
and clear, robust to the taste, yet
we don't pour from fine old kegs for
we hurt from hand, head and legs.
We real people reel under stages
of life. Goodness done with
some fleeting fun shapes
balanced winners. In *The Winter's
Tale* the bard said, *Go together,
you precious winners all.*

Alaska's Colors

… Sentinels of the stillness,
lords of the last lone land.
from "The Pines" by Robert Service

Red is the sea-sky during evening.
White clouds drift toward the dark.
Blue ocean reflects green pine woods.

Red bunch berries sleep on the floor of sub alpine fir forest.
Red bear berries cluster everywhere near the skin and bone sitka spruce.
Red strawberries in a plump patch smile at yellow bulblets of rice lilies.
Red raspberries add a field of fire next to the two-tone butter and eggs.

White lichen, configured like tiny caribou antlers, sit on black boulders.
White topped cotton grass waves its fluffy hats in the wind.
White and purple robed nootka lupine looks regal along the stream.
White hooded Mount Denali majestically towers over wildlife.

Blueberries hang like marbles aside a hot-pink sea of sun baked fireweed.
Blueish gooseberries lie below a field of green-gray caribou moss.
Blue spruce holds its nose as odor rises from the skunk cabbage.
Blue huckleberries dance in the rain around a tall thin birch stand.

SAXOPHONE

A monosyllabic European called Sax
Invents a horn, walla whirley wah, a kind of twisted
Brazen clarinet, but with its column of vibrating
Air shaped not in a cylinder but a cone …

From "Ginza Samba"
by Robert Pinsky

Jazz Quartet

Snare and sock beat the
excitement of tempo.
Alto sax chirps and scales
to high F sharp as
grace notes bounce
off every wall of the studio hall.
Guitar picks up the theme
with strings singing
harmony interlaced
with melody mild.
Double bass undertow
of beat vibrates joy in
the ear of my soul.

Dylan Thomas Resurrected Gives Rise to a Hybrid Poem in a Disjointed Form While Traveling to Greece

I read airy verse while flying cloud high
listening to jazz and Yo Yo Ma
aboard an aircraft bound for ages
older than I, older than most dead.

In the torrent salmon sun ...
At poor peace I sing ...
Seaward the salmon, sucked sun slips ...
From fish to jumping hill!

The Lufthansa stewardess fills my glass
with white wine as I dine. After, I read
poetry of Whitman and Thomas,
both feeding me with quality music.

Only the drowned deep bells
Of sheep and churches noise
Poor peace as the sun sets ...
At God speeded summer's end.

Envy wells up in my soul.

Once a drunk with DT's wrote,
... Hubbub arid fiddle, this tune
On a tongued puffball.

Hands

During Dad's later years
he tends his hands
like some human bird
grooming his feathers.

He touches his care-giving hands
during his time on the ALS cross
until he can no longer raise his arms.
What is he looking for, I wonder?

Are the brown freckles scars of sins, the red
blotches badges of heartbroken times, the black
and blue patches bruises of foolish ventures,
the crusty, split finger ends pointing to his end?

During this last pain-filled year,
Dad, tied to tubes, fails in slow steps.
God in His graciousness
bestows forgiveness.

Now in my later years,
I find I fondle my hands—hands
that heal and hurt loved ones.
Are my sins my aged blemishes?

It's clear to me now that
Dad was inspecting his soul,
pouring over each memory,
waiting for God's welcoming.

Double Haiku

Peaches and cool skin
omitting bubbly fuzz,
are the cream of life.

The true tree of life
is watching a daughter run
in the morning sun.

No Smoking

No more frenetic fag, lilt weed
lost found a jag, while brown spread
band stays for days for foggy
forget-me-nots. Veins pump
bulgy blood bloated into ends
that feel mud-coated.

For days of eons, on numb
nape and corrected cowlick
on and in the cockpit called
brain, on and over obese brow
(they cause cobweb set scowl)
exist a tic, a twitch, a lack of kick.

Out of Sorts

Do you feel out of sorts sometimes?
You know, somewhere in-between,
unbalanced, and not here or there?
Sure you have. I have, too.

It feels like Limbo.
Wait. Limbo is no more,
yet it's a valid word:
a place of uncertainty.

Limbo's demise is good news
for babies not baptized
and worthy non-Christians
who kicked that eternal bucket.

Purgatory sounds unsavory.
Being human, I fear I may be
riding through its gates on a Harley
gunning the pipes to raise eyebrows.

Purgatory is a hell-of-a-lot better
than hell. I suppose guys like Hitler
and certain politicians would be
at home in hell, but not me.

Heaven sounds heavenly:
playing Hearts with Mom and Dad,
laughing at jokes with school buddies,
hugging Sandy and Mary Ann.

To have some fun we can go
to heaven's entertainment arena
and watch those suicide Jihads
frolicking with their virgins.

Love

My heaven includes those I love.
                Ronald Rolheiser

Love, the greatest of the trinity,
dominates the stage of life.
It forgives hurt, omissions,
and acts of evil error.
Love muffles faults, as do a mother's arms,
and allows sinners the warmth of home.

Love, spiritual DNA,
mysteriously heals souls
and links them to other souls
enabling symbiotic holiness,
manifested in family meals,
loyal friendships and shoes for the poor.

Love, given to anyone or accepted
with smiling heart, reserves
a place of honor in God's house.
The rush of God's love,
freely given or received,
defines the portal to heaven.

Love welds people to part of God,
bonds sinner and saint, cleanses
the sinner and promotes saintliness.
It's dressed in humanity
with the touch of a kiss or hug,
each a share of God's grace.

Shooting Father Time

If I owned a shotgun, I'd try to find
that old bum, Father Time, and shoot him.
I know he's holding the Reaper's sickle,
waiting for me to trip down some stairs.
If I find him, I'll put him in a pickle.

Because he's a two-ton gorilla, he thinks
he can scare the crap out of me with his
grim demeanor. I got him figured out:
I'm not going to panic or be buffaloed
by listening to that old knockabout.

More poetry is my answer to that death
dealer, who swings at our knees when
we approach eighty. I'm taking a detour:
if word writing is not enough, I'm going
to blow my sax to impede that vulture.

In the end, I'll be happy to fly up there
and greet all the greats I've missed.
I know others that I love will follow
me, then we all can thumb our nose,
wave our finger at that bearded fellow.

Sinkholes and Tsunamis

The Russian ballerina of death
dances on 2000 graves-to-be.
One hundred miles per hour winds
pitch a wall of water at lives
and levees flooded with surprise.

Water molecules bend and hug
each other, carrying food and poison.
Sinkholes and debris grow along
the Mississippi. People and homes
are gone. Jazz and Creole food
make Cajun love to tourists no longer.

Children lose their schools. People
miss their jobs. Family happiness is
lost on the bayou where mess begets
stress. The Big Easy today remains.
Little gets done, like Guantanamo.

Sycamores

So he ran ahead and climbed a sycamore tree ...
Luke 19:4

A pair of sycamore trees
grew in the front yard
of the house where we raised
our brood of six offspring.
One tree grew straight arrow
into the cloudy sky;
the other grew crooked
by ten degrees,
yet in due time
it climbed star high.

Some in life are never bent badly.
Others have major crooked events.
We call those trials "crosses."
The bent tree grew taller
and stronger than the other tree.

I got twisted like a pretzel
during a mid-life divorce,
ending sick in mind and body,
but over time I became
clear of mind,
strong of body,
apt.

I climbed that tree one gray day
to think about the curves of life
and how God designs trees.
Praise be, I'm not sick any more,
just like that old, tall sycamore.

Sing the Gospel

Choir members enter from the side door,
go to the vestry as the choir leader
scans and shuffles a music score. There
they don red robes with wide white collars.
One by one, they sit in place on their tiers.

Sitting under Saint Joseph's stone image,
this black choir, with some whites, invites
the congregation to sing and engage. Some
members start singing a warm-up hymn
tuning their voices for sacred songs.

Twenty members flow down the side aisle
then back with the priest; all sing
in cadence in a two-step style,
clap in time to the entrance song, *I Shall
Not Be Moved*, while moving.

Kyrie's passion is like moaning
chants from the bowels of ships.
Today the dissonant suffering
changes into holy harmonies
since *The Lord Is Kind and Merciful*.

Swaying and mixing movement and music,
they sing of glory, for Jesus is here.
Responses speak of love and compassion
because we are made in His image,
the same as all our brothers.

This Gospel group sings festive sets:
Alleluia, Alleluia, to announce
the Word that begets balance
in the kingdom to come. Lord,
let all humans rise on high.

O how I love Jesus is sung by spry
pigtailed girls with beads in rowed hair.
Candor choir sings the echo reply
while swaying, clapping and tapping
their feet so we *See What the End Will Be.*

Hosanna high notes sound loud
with syncopated hand-clapping,
give visions of that happy crowd
lined along the road, palms waving,
preparing for an Easter psalm.

Slow tempo *Our Father* makes
a plea, chant-like, with full emotion
of voices filling the church with glory.
The Lamb of God grants us peace and
grace—asks God the same for the world.

Red robes file to take communion,
plaintively, offering a melody of *Taste
and See the Goodness of the Lord.* Then
we all plead for *The Touch of the Lord,*
so someday we can all overcome.

A medley tunes my mind with sweet
reward; holy Mass ends in a joyous mood:
I Say Yes, Lord, Yes and *I Will Trust in the Lord.*
I will *Just Be Praising the Lord* with this collage
of colorful sound, these singing Gospel voices.

The choir sings with the people
a hand holding, foot stomping,
thigh slapping, smile giving, soul lifting
outstanding amen, a *Great Amen.*

A Medley

I'm gonna sit right down
and write myself a poem.
Poets say, write for your readers.
I write to feel more at home.

Somewhere over the rainbow
is a green elf with a chin mole,
who has four missing teeth
and is smiling at his pot of gold.

Fly me to the moon
if a green golf course is there
with crater traps and one mile
holes with tall flag poles.

I've got you under my skin.
Golly, I hope it's not a sin.
You're a young chick, a cute hen.
I'm an old rooster ready to eat crow.

You made me love you,
I didn't want to do it.
Wasn't our love hot
and sweet before we split?

I don't stand a ghost of a chance with you
cause you are so good lookin.'
Those muscular macho men
surely will capture your cookin.'

I don't want to set the world on fire
or create a world flood.
I write my poems because
they're in my lifeblood.

TROMBONE

The brass trombone, clarinet, their jackets,
heavier than electric guitars to me,
the highs, lows, notes of my time …

From "Dancing in Time"
by Mary Simion

Brewing Jazz

Jazz & Dave
  Life breathes an adventure in improvisation.
  Art evolves, as does Brubeck's disciplined freedom.
  His powerful hands energize the path of jazz.

Soldier of Jazz
  Nearly killed during the Bulge, choral music comes to him.
  "The Commandments"—songs of sacred social justice.
  At war's end, Dave's Wolf Pack Band blows Rhine jazz.

Blue Rondo a la Turk
  Time notes Dave's signature, nine beats grouped in eight.
  A family of block chords stamps swinging blues.
  Rondo form makes classic this innovative jazz tune.

Seasoned Quartet
  Desmond, Wright, Morello and Dave make musical history.
  Jones, Moore, Militello and Dave foster current raves.
  A march of musicians through time lights the tree of jazz.

Invent, Create
  Down Beat, Doctorates and music awards honor Dave,
  a grand piano poet, who invents sound-streams of joy.
  Darius Milhaud creates world-healing works through Dave.

Take Five for Six
  Brubeck brews grooves of gigs world-wide
  while playing his fine-tuned love for Iola and
  his four sons, who add more than a pinch of jazz.

My Father Was Lifted

My father was lifted into our God.
There his memory burns our sins it seems.
His soundless pain cries not beneath the sod,
yet tears come when images prompt erratic dreams.

Dad's brittle hurt being and pasted smile
with twist gave us silent faith untimely fed.
His eons placed pain all that while
when his hospital bed was red on red.

Gradually, death by-passed needle and tube.
Life slipped drop by drop, while dominion
rested not upon his shoulders, too weak and nude.
Dad's old veins finally closed—ending pain.

Now forever, Dad, have a good time,
for, dad of mine, you're one of a kind.
No more must you dream in boney pod.
My father was lifted into our God.

Cape Cod Respite

The one room beach cottage, close to the fish market,
provides food and fun. Just what we planned at the onset.
    We use time to rest in the aura of our love.

Fresh blue fish planked on restaurant decks
tastes tangy and renders cheap checks.
    Teach a man to fish and the blues drift away.

Cranberry bogs are like small red seas
where wading men rake around the bees.
    Red berries bob like souls on an ocean.

A bucket of today's shrimp turns orange from gray
when my love boils them for us to eat each day.
    Tiny bites of love beget unity.

The Kennedy compound guarded by woods and wire
stands by a sea of tragedy ending in glory under fire.
    Family joy takes us beyond grief.

Cycling on Martha's Vineyard on a hot day
fatigues us but surges the juice of our play.
    Pain in life teaches lovers kindness.

Black antique cars cry out on the museum floor
for new love, for hands to stroke fender and door.
    Time layers generations—they all seek the touch.

We walk on the Cape beach thick with orange-flecked rock.
I choose ten of these stones for my pond stock.
    A simple joy: a stone held in one's hand.

The cottage next to ours radiates noisy sex.
Life is simple, then we make it complex.
    Life finds a way during our walk in life.

Listening to Igor

Between being a smart senior in high school
and a naive, dumb freshman in college,
I have a summer interval of play and work.
I play in a big band, Kenton and Herman
charts hoping to sound like the Bird.

I work as a city inspector, watching
thick-handed tattooed men sweat while
persuading them to pour concrete to spec.
Getting money for college is my goal.

On weekends, I feel free while listening
to vinyl 78s of Brubeck, Dizzy and Parker
playing bop, jazz idols making cool.
I try to get hep by smoking fags and
playing in local bands to hear teens scream.

Dad, bless his soul, lets me take our
Dodge out to hang with the guys.
Slowly touring Monroe's streets,
I fail to find my pals who are at the
beach, the movies or the pool hall.

I park near the courthouse on
Washington Street, switch on the
low-fi car radio and tune a lot. I find
highbrow music. Classical music isn't
jazz, but how bad can it be, if a hundred
guys play on a myriad of instruments?

I listen to a *Rite of Spring* that
premiered in Paris and caused a riot.
From the first notes from the bowels
of the bassoon to the slashing,
crashing high-noted brass finale,
my mind becomes transfigured.
I become a classical music fan.

Stravinsky's raucous ballad to spring
roars from the open windows of the car.
Promenading townspeople eye the
concert scene with glances of disbelief
and disdain, while I sit in rapture supreme.

Life Is a Bridge

At age nine, I wound a sparrow
with my birthday BB gun.
I put the bird in a shoe box
wishing it to be a bird-hospital.
He takes a day to die.

Sixty-five years later,
a robin hits our window,
full speed. Stunned, he stands
still on the patio a time, watching
me watching him, then flies off
to sing cheerful chirps again.

We sing spiritual hymns or
jazz tunes about social mores,
or love ballads about passing
passion, or jingles about making
money—songs that don't
abet our thirst for happiness.

Love amplifies during life: a
child licks an ice cream cone,
woman cooks chicken soup,
man clears brush and tree,
priest prays for his flock,
musician plays Bartok or Basie.

As we age, wisdom seeps
into us and old eyes see better.
In our last hour, our eyes will
show no fear. My beloved
will leave smiling in a seamless
transition. I'll be barefoot,
perhaps walking on stones.

Together we will lie below,
cold, while in truth we'll fly
here and there warmed
by the breath of God.

We could rest in a shoe box, have
a rock for our heads. It doesn't
matter, for love has dominion.

Pantoum's Windy Tune

Piccolo pitch rides mountain-high
when the orchestra plays the score.
Flute flies and scales the sky,
while musicians massage the melody.

When the orchestra plays the score,
clarinets trill grace notes.
Flute flies and scales the sky,
as musicians laugh with their instruments.

Clarinets trill grace notes.
Oboes vibrate double reeds in double time
as musicians laugh with their instruments.
The audience claps to the beating rhythm.

Oboes vibrate double reeds in double time.
Bassoons sound like a pack of baboons.
The audience claps to the beating rhythm.
Saxophones wail and whine like wind.

Bassoons sound like a pack of baboons.
Piccolo pitch rides mountain-high.
Saxophones wail and whine like wind.
Flute flies and scales the sky.

Arise Dear Sweet, Sweet Sandy

Arise dear sweet, sweet Sandy,
your Light has come.
Rest daughter at His knee;
your night is done.

Sandy stays in my mind shifting.
She is delicate as spun glass;
strong as steel in the arms of Love
she is. She is! She is!!

Come away. Come away death.
Sandy's taken young. Cruel. Unfair.
Fly away. Fly away breath.
No more she endures the petty pace.

All this twists the sinews of our hearts.
Our loved Sandy lived with grace.
Our sadness hurts all our souls, but
remember, remember her sweet face.

Arise dear sweet, sweet Sandy;
your Light has come.
Rest daughter at His knee;
your night is done.

Juxtaposition Due to a Child's Death

Randomly, the cell forces kingdom
come scowl since life is lost making
dogs howl. DNA solutions late make
young kisses on the cheek disappear.
Tomorrow we all have that date.

Life in fathoms vast is matched with
the march of earthly feet doing trillions
of things. Our lives comprise the petty,
the waste, even while God gives balance,
stability, and the love of each of us.

Yet my tears still are not still;
they are not wet, but vibrate
with waves of empty feeling
for rich memories. Eight years
are indeed precious, but not long
in space and time of shifting sands.

The Gun

Dad tells Mom that it's not a big deal:
Junior should have a BB gun
before I take him rabbit hunting.
I agree with Dad and nod my head.

My birthday gift, wrapped with paper
rabbits, squirrels and assorted birds,
radiates hunting. With my Red Rider
BB Gun, I begin my rite of passage.

Practicing in the field behind our garage,
I take aim and, with my first shot, a sparrow
falls to earth. I run to see my trophy kill
and get a queasy feeling in my gut.

Holding the small bird in my trigger hand,
I become concerned for that fluff of feathers,
for the tiny thing heaves in pain,
the left wing is clearly broken.

I rush the wounded avian home to be nursed,
while stress and regret creep inside my head.
Mom aids her evil son by suggesting,
with lots of vocal support, a wing tourniquet.

Two sad days pass before the bird passes.
After a down week, I want to apply my rifle
skills in another field, but I need to practice
a distant shot with a suitable target.

My cousin Hank and friend Floyd
sit down with me to plan a target range
that will be a challenge. A streetlight on
Hollywood Drive is the perfect target.

That light sits as a white wild bird perched
on a pole. To my everlasting shock, my first
shot cracks the cover, crashes the glass to
the street with a terrible, quiet noise.

We flee like scared sparrows.

The Protest

That guy gave me the finger!
My wife looks shocked when a war-hawk
flies by our MoveOn antiwar protest.

At Big Beaver and Rochester Roads,
eighteen-wheelers blast, bugs beep,
and motorcycles rev motors.

Along with toots of *yes yes*, people give
thumbs up, wave hands, flash headlights,
smile and shout *Right on.*

Twenty-six peaceniks hold signs
that disagree with those Bush-birds
in D.C. and the mess they make in Iraq.

Media fly all around us. TV and
newspaper people record us
exuberant advocates for peace.

After one hour of intense antiwar
campaigning, we walk to a local
restaurant for a tasty panini sandwich.

At home that night, we view our efforts
on a 30-second TV spot—me waving my six foot
stars and stripes high above my head.

The voice over has a nasty comment
by a pro-war politician who ticks me off.
I give him a mental bird.

$E = M \times C^2$

Energy equals mass times the speed of
light times the speed of everlasting *Light*.
Einstein's hairy head forms the elegant
nuclear equation and it plays hell
on Hiroshima and Nagasaki.

Nuclear power cedes us killing pain, yet
it's a source for healing humankind—
a killing jolt when conscience is dead,
a saving craft when benevolence is alive.
It paints skin into a blistered rose,
feeds mouths replacing oily blues,
produces paper cranes for Sadako.

Two silver air machines ride the blue wild
yonder delivering Little Boy and Fat Man
that mushroom into two hundred thousand
lost lives, yet two million lives are saved
since Downfall and Y-Day do not occur.

Farm tools revert to normal use.
Weapons became melted piles.
Tears and fears of those polite island
people don't stop the memory of
those lost at Nanking, Pearl Harbor,
Bataan, Guadalcanal, Iwo Jima and Okinawa.

Did that searing hyper flash
show the finger of God
and not just the hand of Man?
Mystical wonders are in God's domain,
for the energy of the cosmos is
designed by the Creator. We are
part of that design, when
Light shines through us.

Death of JFK

In '63, a young engineer designs Saturn missile software while working high-up in the Baronne Building overlooking the quarter in the Crescent City where jazz was born. On the corner of Baronne and Lafayette, Oswald hawks his paper wares. Two weeks later the engineer's phone rings. His wife's voice says, "JFK was shot." Shock floods his mind. Writing code—impossible. "Where's a TV?" Riding the elevator down, two business men discuss the shooting while the engineer wails inside. One man says, "Kennedy can't help his nigger soldiers now." The engineer nearly vomits.

He holds his tongue—controls himself!
He holds his anger—maintains himself!
He blocks his mind—steels himself!
He hails his values—believes himself!

In the bar two blocks away
he nurses two beers
while viewing a blaring TV
and holding back tears.

He imagines those three shots
have surely destroyed Camelot.
Bobby waits in the wings
for his place and burial plot.

Decades later, that engineer
stands still on Arlington's sacred soil
as the flame burns with a soft glow
reflecting again his old turmoil.

Brother Bob was interred
without monument or flame
about a stone's-throw away.

TRUMPET

The music from the trumpet at his
lips is honey mixed with liquid fire.

From "Trumpet Player"
by Langston Hughes

Gibbs' Gigs*

Gibbs' organ trio inflames
Carter's wild saxophone tone.
The Hammond power instrument
lights a counterpoint fire in music.

Sparks start low with a deep bass line.
Foot pedals and bass hand interplay,
conjure images of a sorcerer
toying with lit torches that flame

and spread dramatically
in colored textures in solos.
Swelling, veering and scorching,
block chords deliver with
the sting of Ali's left jab.

*Inspired by Mark Stryker's "Jazz Highlights"
column in the *Detroit Free Press*, 8/13/04

Whoopers

A renegade family of whooping cranes
wanders neighborhoods in Hernando County.
Their true home is the Chassahowitzka
National Wildlife Refuge in Florida
near Crystal River's power plant.

Ker-loo, ker-lee-loo.

Operation Migration with their big bird
flying machine couldn't coax
the 5-foot-tall parents and their chick
to the refuge where other whoopers
just might be jealous.

Ker-loo, ker-lee-loo.

They drink from backyard ponds.
Flower gardens and bird feeders
are their prime feeding targets.
Wildlife agents warn us not to go near
or offer food or friendship.

Ker-loo, ker-lee-loo.

Mom and Pop guard their chick like soldiers—
long necks at attention, beaks ready at all times.
Containing these white feathered
fowls is a neighborhood chore.
They can kill with a single strike.

Has anyone seen little Mary Moore?

Ker-loo, ker-lee-loo.

Fat Cat

The cat chews the earth in great gulps
of sand and stone. She eats grass and weed,
brush and nest, stick and brick. Back
she comes for another bite of ground
and makes mounds of dusty dirt and bone.
She tucks her mouth to drop not a pound.

Fat and squat cat turns to add a new hill,
swings again to gorge and then to cough
upon that spill. She tastes and regurgitates.
Her mouth is like a hippo's eating oft.

While fuming and spitting from her stack,
a hole increases wide and deep.
The cat, like a panzer tank, retreats
on her steel bands, with a beep, beep.

Her yellow fur gets soiled with sod.
Tough turf tears at her teeth through the day.
This one-armed cat dives for a big bite,
sniffs at the pit and chews a mouthful of clay.

She tires and growls no more,
puts down her massive double-
jointed arm and rests for the night.
Tomorrow: double toil and trouble.

The Trainer

My bedroom on Fern Court is little.
That's okay for a boy who is small.
There's a big bed for sleep and rest,
for games and when I'm ill, a closet
for toys, clothes, an oval
rug by the desk and dresser—
both of which hold my treasures.

Only one windowsill, where I sit
viewing wonders of the backyard:
garden full of bumblebees, garage
with my bike and bats, and beyond—
fields and trees, mulberry and
cherry ready to climb.

My window is my door
to the back porch roof, where
I sit at sunsets giving
me the soul of a poet.

I work months to make a model
of a double-winged trainer with
stars on its yellow and blue body.
The wingspan is a yard wide. It's
powered by a thick, rubber band.

Today is the day for my plane's
first flight. We go through the
window-door onto the edge of
the roof. We both are wound up
tight. Up goes the trainer, then
down to earth, crashing into pieces.

For my birthday, Mom got me another
model plane—a single wing racer
with aerodynamic features touted on
the box. This one will fly straight
and be able to survive for a long time.

Smoking Horns

Jazz environs need clearer vision
of polyphonic improvisation
during smoking metal jams that
pack in fans dragging on weeds.
Bright color sounds flow in hazes of gray;
rapid riffs rise in clouds from puffing people.
Musicians blow silver-gold notes
while wrapped in a tobacco shroud.

Phil Woods is an honored
philosopher of the alto.
His sounds now drown
through his emphysemic
pipes, choking breath needed
for lip, tongue and lung.

Must great artists become marred in tar?
Must nicotine mist force the death of Art?

Detroit's famous alto giant,
Larry Nozero, made music of
unfiltered dynamic lyricism.
Now Larry's alto is—silent.
His soul weaves in waves
of jazz with twirls, swirls
and creative curlicues of
sound. Smokes and strokes
have no dominion now.

Cool never again are
cigarettes in hand, while
horns smoke in the band.

WW2 in a B24

I reach high but never out of sight,
searching for the initial point.
God direct me in yonder flight.

Engine three has a bad vapor lock.
The formation flies on not to disappoint.
I reach high but never out of sight.

We have hard flak, wet weather sock.
Both hell and heaven do anoint.
God direct me in yonder flight.

Number four shimmies with a knock,
like a jazz band's counterpoint.
I reach high but never out of sight.

Each mission is a war bird flock,
spewing death to make life disjoint.
God direct me in yonder flight.

I'm alive for my future stock
after sorties of forced appoint.
I reach high but never out of sight.
God direct us in yonder flight.

Veterans' Day

I sit here in the loft among
Christian icons. Candles, beads
and chalice are placed on the table
surrounded by images of Christ.

I'm here to pray for all veterans
alive or dead, ours or theirs.
War is not made by You, but
contrived by simple souls
who fall into a pit of black.

God help the troops who go forth
to the call of duty, wrong or right.
God help the blind or broken
veterans scarred in battle
throughout human history.

Forgive us Thermopylae, Jericho,
Vietnam, Dunkirk, Dresden,
Hiroshima, the rape of Nanking
and Iraq. Forgive us our bloody
sieges, our pots of boiling oil.
Forgive us for killing children.
Forgive us for our madness.
I'm full of sadness.

What's for Dinner?

Artichokes choke me up, but
Belgian waffles, buffalo wings
Carrot cake, apples and
Dungeness crab grab my taste buds.
Eggplant is another favorite.
Flounder, a flat fish,
Grouper, the Cadillac of fish and
Haddock, a cod, are healthy foods.
Ice cream is my creamy delight.
Jam on ice cream tops that taste.
King crab, a horseshoe crab, over
Lettuce lightly iced is nice.
Meat, simmered and placed over
Noodles, fills the tummy and beats fish.
Opossum, in the South, is a super supper.
Pea soup with ham is a winter treat.
Quail, prepared correctly over
Rigatoni makes my mouth water.
Strawberries and cream move people to beam.
Tater Tots are coveted by tots.
Urodele tail is tastier than snail.
Veal is too much cholesterol.
Wheat makes bread for the baskets of the world.
Xylose is a rare sugar.
Yolk of egg makes
Zebra and zucchini tender to the taste.

Without Sanctuary

Our church group, twelve white people,
drives to the Wright Museum in Detroit
for an ordinary social justice event,
which will explore the meaning of *exploit*.

The museum is a cathedral of color-filled
culture, a building with a dome flooding light
onto a mosaic floor to display how
Amistad shipped slaves stacked in blight.

Black is the presence of all colors:
a rainbow of music and poetry.
We view a bloody display of a black—
murdered, hanging dead on a tree.

The exhibit shows decades of violence
in a video, where James Cameron pleas
to God to spare him after two chums
are lynched on limbs of maple trees.

The Ku Klux Klan marks ten thousand
vile voices saying conform or swing.
Blacks are without sanctuary on those
trees, swinging, swinging, swinging.

America is not always beautiful. Images
of blacks cover trees with red black blood.
The poet said only God can make a tree.
White men twisted trees into an evil flood.

Billy Holiday sang songs of black plight.
She moaned a tune called *Strange Fruit*.
Strange trees bear a strange fruit,
blood of the leaves and blood of the root.

Anthropology

The Museum of Anthropology's
plaza sprouts a 50 foot mushroom,
a column that spews a fall of water
that flows over a half dozen
cultures carved on its stem.

The Mexican guide talks of Toltec,
Aztec, Zapotec, Mixtec, Olmec,
and Mayan civilizations, their
ancient artifacts: jars, tools, gems,
skulls impaled with spear heads,
the Sun Stone that tells times
of religious sacrificial rituals.

Juan asks for a volunteer
for a demo of death. My
proximity to him tags me
victim of this bloody deed.

Juan grabs at my arms, legs and neck
as would have five Toltec priests.
Numero *seis* would have used a
sharp glass tool to cut deep into my
chest, then thrust his hand around
my heart, withdrawn it and placed
my beating organ on a dish-altar on
the belly of a reclining stone woman.

I left my heart in old Mexico,
2000 miles from San Francisco.

Portrait of a Poet as an Old Man

Ah, we go into infinity for eternity.
I'll be delighted to be around
for that whole time if I don't get
trapped in a super black hole
bouncing from reality to anti-reality.

It's tough to bide my time when
I've got a decade of life left, if I'm
lucky. To hell with that biding stuff.
I'm going to pump, pry and push-out
as many poems as my pencil will allow.

The woods behind our backyard
beckon me each spring to walk
among winter's broken trees, gleaned
by God's law as pegged in science.

When I'm culled by nature, I hope
the Designer will open the same door
that Martin asked to be opened in '68
when he said the day before he died:

I am a sinner like all God's children.
But I want to be a good man.
And I want to hear a voice saying
to me one day, 'I'll take you in and
bless you, because you tried.'

When I Write My Wild Poems*

When I write my wild poems
as the searing sun burns
in day, or when, in drab night
the heat in my brain bakes
lovers and loners in their dreams,
I use my pen to paint nocturnes
to exercise part of God that makes
wisdom with words, ink and schemes,
not for ego by lectern light
but for folks of prosaic sight
to quell their grievous groans.

Being proud of words in poems
bears no rage that turns
the reader into rapid flight
from these fevered songs
which mean nothing to the dead,
but stir loves and themes
to allay sadness and fright,
to cause the drab night bright
if they but heed my wild poems.

*Parallel Poem from *In my Craft or Sullen Art*
by Dylan Thomas in "Selected Poems 1934–52"

VIBRAPHONE

… Pipho's vibes simmer in the fetching harmony and catch fire.

From *Detroit Free Press*,
"Detroit Artists Link Jazz, Church"
by Mark Stryker

An Evening with Sonny

Sonny walks onto the stage with a limp
wearing multicolored grab—red pants,
purple shirt, green vest, flashy
snippets in tones of his jazz.

Rollins, a master in the school of Bop,
feeds his horn food beyond a fixed diet.
His clever music creates mountains
of jazz mania with intelligent fun.

No creamy purr from Sonny's horn.
No scaly scales to bore one's soul.
No liquid long notes that lack knack.
No sterile sounds that rap time.

Absorbing a Rollins concert burns
joy in our hearts, fuses jazz figures
into our minds and impacts our ears
with a Joycean stream of musical prose.

Critics claim Sonny is a Colossus of Jazz,
pushing music through his curved conical tube
in unending figures of delight and surprise,
creating new twists within every tune.

His sextet plays sensual jazz
in Ann Arbor for the academic crowd.
Sonny's support talent amplifies
his sun-filled saxophone.

The sun image sums his art up, nicely:
Whole round notes, riffs of hard grace,
phrases to force grins, bright staccato
highs, honks and wails, trills and thrills.

At concert end comes the deafening
sound of hands meeting hands,
which forces eyes to beam behind
shades with sparks and tears.

Rollins tries to cross the stage to exit
by the wrong door. A sidekick gently holds
his arm, guides him to the proper retreat.

Where Did My Sister Go?

As youngsters we are close,
like lines of poetry. Me nine,
she six, a team, a mix, playing
games, having tiffs over toys.

In the field behind our garage
a neighbor has a brush bonfire.
We watch while it burns out.
I jump over the dying embers
and she with bare feet follows,
landing in the center of the cinders.
I carry her home where Mom
tearfully bandages her feet.

I, a new teen, and she, not yet ten,
go our ways. Younger brother Paul,
subs for me. They become
a new team: play, ride bikes
and bug each other in fun.

Big band jazz captures my ears
in these teen years with sounds
of Kenton and Herman playing
on the family phonograph.
She likes pop stars and soft ballads
on that argued-over machine.

Senior I, freshman she, are
worlds apart, different schools.
Already boys knock at the door.
Like panting puppies, my buddies
show interest in our family treasure.
Already Mary Ann knows
the rainbow promise of life.

Contact slackens when jobs
and family duties dilute our
childhood warmth. We have
flashes of fun during family affairs,
watch our kids run. Card games,
embellished with sliced bananas in
Jell-O, jell our joy and fill memories.

Now we walk near eternity.
One of us writes poetry
to squelch fear, dampen anger.
The other drains brain cells and
stares into a pallid place as synapses
snap into emptiness.

Memories soothe my mind:
I see flying blond hair,
a girl curling on her trike
doing a tight figure eight.

Driving through Mississippi

Bust Bircher Barry. Vote for L.B.J.
read the banners I placed on the side panels
of our packed Chrysler station wagon.
We leave the South, where white rules the night.

Crossing Lake Pontchartrain,
we head into redneck terrain:
Picayune, Hattiesburg and Meridian,
where the kids will get their fuel.

In Laurel, people parade for Barry.
Bands and cheerleaders lead
a herd of white locals, acting loco.
A miniskirted gal taps our window,
Y'all vote for Goldwater!

We drive on to Columbus and Tupelo,
where, nearby, Faulkner wrote southern stories
and Elvis started his hips gyrating.
We stop at a seedy Booneville motel.

A beat-up red truck with a hound
in the bed and a rifle hanging on a rack
is parked a few units away.
Three men eyeball the unwelcome banners.

My kids help me carry our gear
into the room, which looks dismal.
I remove the banners, tossing them
in a trash can, glancing at the men.

Holding the phone in my hand,
I sleep uneasy in that pigpen.
Perhaps I'm some kind of idiot,
but I would do it again.

First Friends

Fern Court is not courtly: two
strings of houses tucked closely
side by side on a dead end,
ending on the back of a two-car
garage on another street.

I live in the first house on the left.
In my child's eye, I tell my mind
my domain is cool living, a
place where kids thrive, play
kick the can, war with cap and
rubber guns and hide and seek
using tree, field or bush.

My best Court friend is Floyd Bert,
whose parents own the corner store.
He actively supplies treats from the
glass candy display cabinet.
Root beer in small wax containers
pleases my taste buds the most.

We build model airplanes,
take in matinees of *The Shadow*
and Tom Mix saving the schoolmarm.
We eat lush black bing cherries
from a tree that a rich man
deems off limits to our gang.

My other best friend is Barbara
Baker, who is one year older than I.
She is the only child of Doctor
Baker and plays the violin.
Barb knows a lot. We play
with our gang for hours.

One summer day, Barb and I
decide to do a forbidden thing, hide
behind some tall thick bushes next
to a neighbor's shed. I show her
my thing. She graciously shows me
hers. Then we run to our homes,
she giggling, me laughing.

Thank You, Matt

A teacher of jazz piano is
honored by his students
at the Jazz Forum with a quality
quintet gig that we really dig.

Matt's Jazz Studies at Wayne State
shapes artists who play today moon
high with instrumental joy and soul—
snappy chords, juicy harmonies with
triplets singing and solos wailing.

Pipho tickles his vibes and our toes.
Gwinnell flies over the ivories, eagle-like.
Prout plucks his guts with clever figures.
Winn wins fans with tricky skin solo beats.
Collins blows twisty scales with wizard skill.

Matt smiles as he starts his own tune
sitting kingly on his piano bench throne.
The notes of his musical delight coax
the crowd to cheer. A grand honor indeed.

The Apple Orchard

The backyard pond near our garden
has a vine-gated entry that leads
into woods. All seasons invite me
to stroll through that arched gate
to the wilderness, a golden goal.

My grandchildren and I cut a path
through the woods for trips to see
snakes, fox, deer and frogs in bogs.
Oh, the green; it's so excellent,
a carpet of warm woven love.

The woods once held a lush apple orchard
that now lies in decay with limbs broken,
trunks split. Stately oaks and wild cherry
stand in their place. Fields and dells
with grassy hills append the trees.

We walk and witness transformation,
sad at first but a sacred cosmic rite that
flows into being by God's creative might.
The children laugh and poke at bugs,
bask in nature with innocent delight.

We return to yard's edge where stands
one last productive apple tree. On the ground
lie small red spheres for deer.
This last tree-soul seems so sensitive
in doing its good without any fear.

Christmas Sense

*for Brother Remigius Bullinger, CSC**

A new baby bundle smells good,
like hot soup on a cold day. Infant
Jesus brings love of brotherhood.

A baby is smooth to the touch,
like the silk robes of the three kings.
Infant Jesus feels pain from every crutch.

A baby tastes the milk of life
as does the lamb that lies on straw.
Infant Jesus tastes and sees our strife.

A baby listens and yearns to learn,
like a student aching for knowledge.
Infant Jesus hears our pleas and concerns.

A baby's wide eyes see the light
like a night owl's visible wisdom.
Infant Jesus sees our plight by holy sight.

* My high school English teacher, who wrote poetry,
including a Christmas poem each year.

Brotherly Love

You have been a caring and helpful
brother to me, when I was small,
when I was in high school and now.
I'm proud of your accomplishments.
I love you.
        Paul Van Slambrouck, Ph.D.

My one, lifetime, always, best pal
spoke of Mom while we drank some beers.
This he quickly told to his Sal. We
both wanted to stop Mom's tears
through those hard years of her sad plight
when Dad suffered and then passed on.

Today, we have increased insight,
enhanced spirit and a firm bond. We
toast to the finer, purer parts
of our values, which we work at, planting
the best into the hearts of our
children. We both stand pat in love.
We both have a passion to give
our wives in true fashion.

Bird Battle

Twelve boulders sit serenely,
defining the borders of two ponds.
Flowers, ground vines, evergreens
and rocks with veins of colored ice
encircle the ponds like a fort.

Stocked with orange carp, blue
shubunkin and woods frogs, the ponds
brew new life links every spring.
Water lilies light both surfaces with
bright yellow, pure white and rosy pink.

Patio sitters drink white wine
while nodding yes to each other.
Sunsets shine onto the pond. Fish
schools yawn for food. Frogs
jump at flying bugs. Watching
life, life is good.

Aerated water and chemicals
maintain a healthy fleet of fish,
yet when we stroll by their domain,
fish scoot away in a paranoid swish.

Next day I wake to a squawking sound.
Peeking through the window pane, I
see him—Big Bird, blue gray,
not Sesame Street yellow, and
a beak like a fisherman's spear.

I see five fat carp gobbled
by that bandit from the sky.
A pond net?—bad for esthetics.
A water gun?—we'd all get wet.
A pellet gun?—against the law.
But fishing line around the ponds
could give Big Bird the bird.

Landing in the backyard, Big Bird
strolls over to one of the ponds.
Spooked with fear of the line,
he takes off screeching. The
fish swim with happiness,
frogs return to hop again,
pond-sitters click their glasses.

Next spring, nature puts a kink in our lines.
Big Bird has sired five hungry bandits,
whose attacks come in fearless waves.
Goodbye spring crop of small fish.
Young birds beat us by ducking the lines.

Five miniature herons are victors
over humankind, but the fight continues
with a new line strung low to the ground.

Can Big Bird cope with the mind of man,
explorer of DNA, traveler of the cosmos,
inventor of the microchip and computers?
We'll see what the damn pecking order is.

Bastogne

The Battle of the Bulge was the largest in WW2
for American troops. Arthur Van Slambrouck,
age 20, my cousin, was killed when 6000 US
troops died within the first two hours.

Parents fear that time of history
that enfolds their son,
a boy who loves life.
As a foot soldier
in the march to freedom
he hears the beat
of war's humdrum drum.

Near Bastogne, a bulging battle
begins in winter's blue death
under cover of fog and snow.
Bullets spew in that inferno.
Bodies bend grotesquely from
foot to head; arms poke the sky.

A star structure sits there today
with names of past friends and foes.
Flags fly to belie the terror
and bravery of those icy days.
Panzers and pistols are there,
not souls of soldiers,
yet still they blaze.

I climb on top of that Belgium star
one warm morning in '92.
With tears, I pray for that dead boy,
like a big brother to me. That
December battle leads me
to scream at the madness
of 50 million dead plus one.

Endangered Species*

Where are the friendly ferret
and the pesky parrot?
Where are the slippery seal,
the putrid bile of the crocodile,
the butterfly that sails the sky,
or the ancient pelican on a glide
or the garter snake with slinky hide?

Where are the ocelots that jump a lot
and the condor that we so adore?
Where are the good scout trout
and Mr. Caribou (we care for you),
or the panting panther
the piping plover
the frog in the bog?

Perhaps one day we'll pay a fee
to see an ancient manatee.

* The United States Postal Service pictured
these animals on its1996 issue of 15 stamps
titled "Endangered Species."

Words

In the beginning was the Word, and the Word
was with God, and the Word was God.

John 1:1

When I become flesh in my mother's womb,
I become part of my God's love, which
guards me then and when, at three, I trot
across our street to meet Dad coming home
from the paper mill. Mid-street a Buick hits
me square. Its tire rolls over my frame
embedding stones in my body, bending
my ribs, forcing pain that ends with a
baby-teeth bite, nearly severing my tongue,
allowing me to moan not a word.

Sister Mary Gerard speaks of John's poetic
prologue in grade school, giving me a rush
of wonder. Brother Remigius speaks of
Hamlet's *words, words, words* in high school,
giving me the thrill of poetry.

Through Him, my flesh becomes six words,
the names of my children. Through Him, I find
Diane—she becomes the word *love* for me.

The hematologist drills my hip to capture
marrow to discover if I'll have tomorrows.
Shaking her head, thinking leukemia, she
withdraws my miniscule white count.
Father Jack's hands hold my hip while
praying words to Him who multiplies loaves
and counts. I feel the warmth of healing.

Years pass full of family, fun
and a retreat into retirement,
blessing me with time in the sun.
Through Him, I write words praising
and thanking Him for the gifts
of poetry, family and life.

VOCALIST

Voice of muted trumpet,
cold brass in warm air.

From "Song for Billie Holiday"
by Langston Hughes

CD Player*

Forever Parker flexes his reed.
His melodic music fills my need.
Be bop sha bam.

Adolf's invention of saxy sound
drowns the war drums
and nourishes our minds.

We kill the Fatherland's illness
by dumping dissonance from above,
while Miller plays *In the Mood.*

Now Illinois Jacquet blows in Berlin
better than a baboon on a bassoon,
better than Richard wishing for a horse.

While the Bird flies around the room,
I listen to his electronically made tune
with its grace, note after note.

*Parallel Poem from *Victrola*
in "Jersey Rain" by Robert Pinsky

Baseball

Dad took me one summer day
to Briggs Field in '41 to see
Joe DiMaggio play left field.
My first Major League game.
That year, Joe took MVP
and the Tigers by their tails.
Sitting in the left field stands,
I yelled at Joe to miss a catch.
I guess that pissed him off;
he didn't hit his homer to me.

The Oakland A's were a hot club in '71
with their bright green and tan uniforms.
My brother and I took my boys to
witness the glory of Reggie Jackson,
whom we often booed with zest.
We sat near first base line waiting
for a foul-ball prize. The A's won.

Ted and Millie were our guests
when the California Angels invaded
Tiger Stadium. The Angels carried bats,
but no harps. Millie, my mother-in-law,
thought the '86 Tigers were saintly.
Saint Walt Terrell had a no-hitter
going in the ninth when Wally Joyner,
an evil Angel, came to bat and hit a single.
A massive sigh arose but we were still
on a high as our Tigers won.

In '04, son Victor invited us to a
Tiger game in Detroit's new park.
The pristine park knocked our socks off
as well as Chicago White Sox socks.
During the second inning stretch, Vic
proposed to Shawn, our daughter to be.
He appeared on one knee on the park's video
screen along with our joyous screams

Being Custer

On his horse of stone,
he sits proudly, even arrogantly.
General Custer, Monroe's Sioux fighter,
steadily holds his steed, shows
control over the war beast.

It's the forties, and he sits in a park
along with pigeon droppings.
Children play cowboys and Indians
around his horse's legs,
kill ghosts of Indians past.

Boys drinking homemade wine
drift into the park one evening.
One lad believes himself as high as
Custer and climbs to sit with him.
He hugs the horse's head.

Elevated by wine, the boy
stands over the horse's neck
as daring as those at Little Big Horn.
He jumps onto the green ground
landing two-footed in triumph.

What becomes of that brash boy?
Is he now a family man, lover,
loner, gambler, or priest?
Perhaps he's the mayor of Monroe.

Alabama in '62

Governor Wallace stands blocking
a Huntsville School door, while white
townspeople stand glaring at black students
waiting for federal agents to clear a path.

A few miles away, a static test of a
Jupiter missile engine shakes the ground,
vomits fire over concreted land and wall.

Our black maid, Jeanette King, cares
for our four small children. Her dollar
per hour salary hardly pays for chicken
pot pie she feeds her family of nine.

Guidance digital circuitry assures
moon shots more certainty of circulation.
Programming software covers my guilt
of paying Jeanett's slave wages.

Ms. King rejoices over her dollar raise,
prompting her to ask other rocket
workers for the same. My coworkers
frown, use silent slurs and curt burrs
to put me in my Yankee place.

Class of 1948

Forty-four green-eared boys started
high school, seeking illumination,
acting like a pride of young tigers.
Our geeked charter class begins with English,
math and science. Brothers of the Holy Cross
mold our reason and do the job of Job,
directing our freshman behavior
toward obedience to book and God.

Sophomores lack wisdom. We prove that
in classes of Latin, music and literature.
Tiger, tiger burning bright in the stillness of the night.
A plethora of sports begin in earnest:
foot, base, volley, basket, tennis: we have a ball.
Our bodies burn like a furnace during games.
Play to win. Use your brain. Stand tall.

Juniors are fun beings, never drab.
We Falcons are an active brood:
The Drama Club dispenses arsenic laced with laughter.
The Dance Band blows like eager beavers in a mood.
The Glee Club sings tender tunes to Kentucky babes.
We earn extra credit by smiling
at the girls of the nearby academy.

On top of the mountain, seniors see everything.
We quote Plato, Faraday and Aquinas.
We are smart, but know nothing,
novice scholars with lofty thoughts
sandwiched between bits of bull.
We walk the walk of Elgar's
pompous tune and, to our dismay,
find that freedom came too soon.

Four score years make us seriously senior.
We become members of the social fabric
of the Creator's world. We've been soldiers
and peacemakers, sinners and saints,
lovers and fathers, poets and players.
Our finest God-given joy, our families,
enable our dreams to be, again and again,
through our children's children
into the dance of infinity.

Cantering into Heaven

Even at eleven, Melissa rides
with majestic poise. At seventeen,
she is a free spirit: tall on saddle,
head held high, jumping with grace.
At twenty-seven, the gates become higher.

Artistry appears in her dressage
that radiates elegance. Her
metal is tested in many ways
producing championship days.
Horse and equestrian become
a harmony of oneness.

The trails and trials of life end
and lead to a field of splendid
symmetry, where riders on horses
gallop unencumbered.

Melissa rides not on earthen paths,
but above, cantering on clouds.
She rides bareback through
trees and meadows, jumping
over gates of pearl. She travels
in God's green pastures,
riding in infinite freedom.

Reconciliation

One hundred miles from Geneva,
as the raven flies, lies Taize
among soft French hills and vineyards.
After the horror of World War Two,
Swiss born Brother Roger
comes to tiny Taize to rejuvenate
the world's youth with a spirit
of love and reconciliation.

Admirers feel his holiness.
His words of love radiate
world wide on the web in
panoramic prayers. Ecumenical
healing with practical deeds
and spiritual services energizes
our souls. Popes, since John 23,
visit Taize to pray with the humble
Lutheran brother. The Polish Pope
gives Brother Roger the Body of Christ.

Brother Roger guides our Taize
reflection: we pray, sing, meditate
and communicate in the silent sound
that strengthens our lives. Taize
prayer brings trust, inner-glow, and
love that sustains and survives.

At 90, Brother Roger dies while praying
surrounded by children and followers,
saints and sinners. A hand holds a
knife that thrice thrusts into his neck.

Cardinal Ratzinger writes that the Designer
creates intelligence, and Father de Chardin
writes that humankind is an ongoing
force of evolving good sense.

Dad's Patio Chair

How to say father and be small
and mean it again.
From Stephen Dunn's "Local Time"

His chair sits stoically in my backyard.
Its cracked wooden slats
and heavy metal frame
push into wet spring soil,
damp as his grave at Roselawn.

Dad sat on that throne-like chair
daily reading the *Detroit Free Press*,
smoking his King Edward cigar.
I could understand if he'd died
of cancer—but not crippling ALS.

This spring warm day, I sit still
on these hard slats, looking
at cracks on my arms and hands
and those on the chair's wooden arms.
Dad's arms dominated the chair's arms.

On my lap lies a Stephen Dunn
book of poetry: *Local Time.*
This chair-time brings Dad near.
Dunn's words perk memories of us
playing catch and hunting rabbits.

We scouted in glades near cornfields,
watched our dog, Jack, kick-up pheasants.
Resting against a tree trunk in silence,
we waited for a squirrel to show,
Jack at our feet eyeing us.
I glanced at Dad's arms holding his 12 gage
and then at my small arms.

Uplifting

Our church is in the round—
like a Greek amphitheater,
only completely circular
with an altar in the center.

On this windy November Sunday,
my eyes are diverted outside by
leaf-dancing entertainment in a
corner of this church in the round.

Brisk winds coax dried leaves
to pile up in that catchall nook.
God's nature dismantles that
rabbit or rodent-leaved bed.

A tiny tornado peals layers of
multicolored leaves, spins
them skyward, mesmerizing my
mind. Up goes a ton of leaves.

Wide windows next to the roof
reveal those leaving leaves,
blown by a stiff west wind
to God knows where.

It's like our prayers going up
to God, to spread grace,
wind-wide, over Mother Earth.
That brings me back inside.

Woods Walking

Mikey and sister Sarah scream
with delight when I announce
we will walk the woods
on this crisp October day.

(Over the years, with the help
of grandkids, I've chopped a path
through our woods to a clearing
where a carrot pile appears each fall.)

The kids, son Mike and I troop
this path and find, here and there,
red berries hanging like tiny
Christmas tree lights.

No carrots or munching deer,
so we move into heavy underbrush
under old apple trees and oaks
holding leaves in their arms.

Over hill, berm, ditch and mound, we
trudge like buffalo, chatting louder than
crows overhead. We step over a fallen
tree that has white fungi on its bark.

We truck on, cross a dirt road onto a
glade, with a border of huge trunks cut
in chunks. The kids climb them to view
a waving field of reeds and grasses.

What is that thing, Dad? We squint
to spy the thing and gawk at a portable
hot tub. Mike photographs the kids
sitting on the blue-marbleized tub.

At supper, I tell them that the woods-elves
were to take their evening bath about now,
but they know we found their hot tub and
are taking the tub deeper into the woods.

Antiquarian Book Fair

Holy Moses, some of these books cost
thousands. The small cubicles line the
coliseum, like dealers in Las Vegas.
They are ducks in rows quacking
about their wares of words.

The brochure lists over a hundred used-book
dealers selling first editions, prints, cookbooks,
books about space, jazz and poetry. I'm looking
for the last three and find three within budget.

I pick-up "Blues for All the Changes" by Nikki
Giovanni (love to speak her name). It's autographed.
The dealer knows her, says she shimmies like her
poems and is known as the Princess of Black Poetry.

I find an Archibald MacLeish, not autographed,
in fine lyrical condition, a '68 first printing.
At my age, the title jumps at my eyes—
The Wild Old Wicked Man. I didn't know
Archie, but he has a poem titled *Cummings.*
Old e. e. was a favorite in my youth.

One of my granddaughters, Sandy, age 10,
made me a book of her poetry. What a
rush for an old poet. I spot John Ciardi's
The Reason for the Pelican.
Oh, how her face will shine.

"Goodbye Could Last a Long, Long Time"

is prophetic and a long title for a jazz tune,
the last cut on Donald Walden's CD,
A Portrait of You. Don passed his horn
to others a few Sundays ago, yet his jazz
echoes through the halls of Oberlin, Michigan,
Michigan State, and jazz joints throughout
our peninsula that have great lakes of music.

Don remains an icon of Bop culture. Disregard
the silence of his golden tenor for his spirit
remains in the soul of jazz as does Hawkin,
Webster, Jacques and Coltrane when they
blow *The Bluebird of Happiness* during
paradise gigs.

Don's mantle of songs, his tunes of life,
permeate the hands of young artists—
the neo-jazz musical genius. The Cardinal
chirps and swings and Christopher Wren
wails with prolific zeal those notes of joy.

In a yuppie basement bar in Birmingham,
Don's trio battles the noise of guys hitting
on gals smoking stogies and squealing
at off-color jokes that drown his clever
sounds. We wait for the break to tell him
of the excitement his music brings to us
even through the chaotic chatter. For the
next set, Walden creates innovative riffs
of jazz-laughter in front of our small table.

Six Wonders

John 14:13

In our world of wonders, I'm a blessed
father responsible for six. My wonders
are God-sent into being, crystals that
radiate comfort and love that I store
in my heart. Yes, they play music
for my soul, and I listen with an open
heart that beats within their being.

Katherine, a queenly name for a daughter,
delivers love daily to her parents and
children, the subjects of her upbeat love.
A daughter, as does a son, brings
glory to her father and her loved ones.
She codes awe into life, programs the
present to help family and friends.

Beth Angela bears a biblical name
given to her by me, lives her love for
all humans, as does Christ, who resides
in these six wonders. A trip to Guatemala
to build a church brings her joy, as does
giving tender warmth to her family. Beth
fills needs with the social gospel of Jesus.

Philip, first son, with the name of biblical
love, sings songs of God's love and
life's good deeds. Phil fishes the Tennessee
River, while his heart beats freely for souls
of poverty who strive to survive. He travels
life on a bike of values that feeds God's
people with hearty meals of happiness.

Michael, strong like the archangel, becomes
a family man late in life with the birth of
his namesake. Mike's love and sensitivity
flows over friends—everyone he touches.
He excels in kindness, even when events
go south, for he understands the value of
living in God's light in the arms of our love.

Victor holds my middle name as his first,
which becomes greater as time tells the
good Vic does. He is the guardian of
family, the worker who provides and
gives to those who are lucky to come his
way. *Be slow to anger and fast to help* rules
Vic during his life. I thank God for him.

Edward has the excellent name of his father,
his son and his grandfather. He loves with
humor, using the tools of a jester, makes his
son and daughter laugh in his love. He carries
love in his heart, which he opens to those who
need a laugh in life. Ed's the dessert of our
family. He says I saved the best for last.

ABOUT THE POET

Edward Van Slambrouck has written poetry at a prolific pace during his "literary-ripe" retirement years. He wrote poems sporadically prior to retirement, since six children and eleven grandchildren put loving constraints on his spare time. As a young engineer, he worked in the aerospace industry, which included computer programming for the moon rocket, Saturn. Later, he was brought on staff at Oakland University (Michigan) as a computer specialist, creating library systems and research tools and teaching some courses in computer science. He was also employed by General Motors Corporation at central office data processing. He completed his engineering career by establishing a computer training company, KETEC Inc. Time was limited during his working years. Nevertheless, he continued to pursue the love-task of writing poetry throughout his adult life. Mr. Van Slambrouck is member of The Academy of American Poets and of The Poetry Society of Michigan.

In addition to writing poetry, Mr. Van Slambrouck plays his alto saxophone almost daily, "to keep tuned to the music of life." During his youthful adulthood, he played saxophone in big bands (charts by Kenton, Herman and Basie) and in combos (five or six musicians). He sang in church choirs, both modern and classical scores, including Gregorian chant. Also, he has been a lover of classical music and an avid aficionado of the original American music form, jazz.

OnSpring: A Family of Poems, Mr. Van Salmbrouck's first book, a chapbook, was published in 2005. Peter Meinke, a noted national poet, commented the following about his chapbook: "… thanks for sending me your touching chapbook, *OnSpring*, whose pages are heartfelt, moving, linguistically admirable and playful."

Mr. Van Slambrouck lives in Orion, Michigan with his wife, Diane. He is 77 years old. He can be reached at vanslam30@yahoo.com. He says "Life is short, and it's good to have a long reach."

ABOUT THE EDITOR

Margo LaGattuta, 2005 winner of The Mark Twain Award for her contribution to Midwestern Literature, has her MFA from Vermont College and four published collections of poetry, *Embracing the Fall, The Dream Givers, Noedgelines,* and *Diversion Road.* Her poetry and essays have been published in many national literary magazines and anthologies. She has done writer-in-the-schools residencies and teacher in-service sessions, both locally and nationally, for 20 years and edited eight anthologies for small presses. In 2002/2003 she received a Michigan Creative Artist's Grant from ArtServe Michigan to complete her newest poetry collection, *Bears Are Taught To Use Cameras.* A two-time winner of the Midwest Poetry Award and many National Federation of State Poetry Societies Awards, she was nominated by Naomi Shihab Nye for a Pushcart Prize for her work in small press publishing. Margo is Associate Editor for *Suburban Lifestyles* in Rochester, where she writes a weekly creative nonfiction column, articles and theater reviews. She teaches writing at University of Michigan-Flint, Baker College and Oakland Community College and conducts creative writing workshops both locally and nationally.

Contact her for more information on workshops or editing at lagapvp@aol.com or www.inventingtheinvisible.com.

ABOUT THE ARTIST

Earl Newman is the artist-printmaker who created the model for the front cover of *Heart Music*.

Early in his career, Mr. Newman traveled to Venice, California with his wife and two children. His work was valued in the Venice environment, and he became well known to art connoisseurs in the area.

Mr. Newman is a prolific producer of art through the medium of silk-screening, also known as serigraphy. He reproduces his designs in volume, usually 100 at a time. This technique is like producing 100 distinctive canvases since he uses different colors of papers and inks. He varies the color blends throughout the run. No two prints are alike.

Besides doing posters for the Monterey Jazz Festival, he does theater posters for the Oregon Shakespeare Theater and Oregon State University. He has an extensive portfolio of nature prints, original sketches, paintings and posters.

The Smithsonian's Division of Musical History in Washington D.C. has acquired a complete collection of his numbered/signed edition of the Monterey Jazz Festival posters since in 1963.

There is a complete list of his jazz posters as well as other posters on his web site: www.earlnewmanprints.com.

Mr. Newman holds a BFA from Massachusetts College of Art and an AMT from Harvard University Graduate School.

Printed in the United States
127560LV00003B/178-246/P

9 780595 478606